HOW TO SET UP A
FREELANCE
WRITING
BUSINESS

HOW TO SET UP A
FREELANCE
WRITING
BUSINESS

An **Insider Guide** to setting up and running
your own copywriting business

JASON DEIGN

howtobooks

For Áine

Published by How To Books Ltd,
Spring Hill House, Spring Hill Road, Begbroke
Oxford OX5 1RX, United Kingdom.
Tel: (01865) 375794. Fax: (01865) 379162.
info@howtobooks.co.uk
www.howtobooks.co.uk

First edition 2003
Second edition 2008

978 1 84528 257 8

British Library Cataloguing in Publication Data.
A catalogue record for this book is available from the British Library.

Cover design by Baseline Arts Ltd, Oxford
Produced for How To Books by Deer Park Productions, Tavistock, Devon
Typeset by Kestrel Data, Exeter, Devon
Printed and bound by Cromwell Press Ltd, Trowbridge, Wiltshire

Contents

Acknowledgements

Several people contributed their experience and knowledge to make sure this book was a far better volume than it could otherwise have been. Julian Goldsmith, for example, provided valuable input into the section on serviced offices. Gareth Llewellyn allowed me to share his cash flow nightmares with readers. Anne Massey of The Editorial Consultancy gave me masses of help with Chapter 11; any and all useful advice in that chapter is entirely thanks to her unparalleled knowledge of direct marketing. Sion Portman took time out from being one of the hottest web producers in the UK to review Chapter 13. Mike Stone's input was invaluable in drafting Chapter 10, and any remaining shortcomings in that section of the book are purely because I was not able to make all the changes he suggested. Tanya Stratton, in particular, deserves a massive thank you for casting her expert eye over Chapters 2 and 5 and the section on IR35 in Chapter 4. All their input into this book highlights a point that I may not have made enough of elsewhere: no matter how much you think you know about a subject, it is always best to get a real expert to check your material.

Finally, I would also like to thank the people at Pfizer Consumer Healthcare for letting me use their ad in Chapter 10, and Jutta Degener for the 'dangerous words' in Chapter 13.

Preface

This book is aimed at anyone who fancies making money from writing – whether on a part-time basis, as a stop-gap measure between jobs, or as a full-time career. No matter which of the above categories you fall into, if you are going to go it alone you will need to know the basics of running a business – or risk the wrath of the taxman, at the very least.

Besides knowing the basics of your trade – in other words, how to write well for the audiences you will be addressing – being successful and making money depends on winning business and keeping clients happy, so I have devoted specific sections of the book to this topic.

Core elements of this book will also, I hope, be useful to people who wish to earn money from writing but do not intend to run their own business. The rules of good writing that I have set out in the second part of the book apply just as much to in-house or agency copywriting as they do to freelance practitioners. Furthermore, in my experience – and that of colleagues in the trade – it is highly likely that even the most sought-after copywriting employee may have to make do on their own from time to time, for example as a way of getting onto the first rung of the employment ladder, overcoming periods of unemployment, supplementing income, breaking into new fields and so on.

Lastly, there may be many people in the creative, marketing and media-related industries who would not consider themselves copywriters but who, I believe, might find elements of this book useful. For people in the public relations industry, for example, I have included information – drawn from both a PR and journalist's perspectives – on how to write press releases, backgrounders and other materials. Web designers might like to take note of my tips on writing for the internet if they are asked to provide copy for the sites they produce. For in-house marketers charged with overseeing internal communications, there are details on how to put together house style guides, packaging corporate messages and so on.

What this book cannot do is cover in detail all the writing techniques and processes in major marketing and media industries such as advertising, direct mail, public relations or journalism. What I have tried to do, instead, is provide some background and some basic tips that will help the novice writer approach projects in these fields. Each of these subjects has been written about by experts far more qualified in their fields than I am and, where possible, I have listed their works in this text for those who wish to delve further.

The first section of this book – up to Chapter 8 – is about the essentials of running a copywriting business. It covers getting started, what equipment you need, how to decide where you should work, what you need to do to keep on top of your accounts and, crucially, how to find work and keep it. If you do not intend to set up in business and instead are using this book as a source of reference on copywriting, then you can skip this section and go straight to Chapter 8.

Chapter 8 is the most important chapter in this book. It deals with the basic skills and knowledge you need to apply to become a successful copywriter.

Chapter 8 onwards is about copywriting itself: what you need to know to write good copy and how you can adapt your style to suit different types of work, from advertising to sales promotion. Finally, at the end of the book, from Chapter 17, there is additional information for practising copywriters. It covers less common types of copywriting work, such as speeches and technical documents, and how you can extend your business into related areas such as marketing and communications consultancy.

Information in some chapters, such as those covering taxation and the cost of equipment, is subject to change. While I have made every effort to make sure details are accurate at the time of going to press, do take care to ensure you get the latest facts from the sources listed at the end of this book and elsewhere.

Note from the Author

In 1996 I gave up my full-time job working in a public relations agency to start my own business as a copywriter.

In the years that followed, my work has been more diverse, interesting, satisfying and rewarding than ever before. Since I am my own boss, I no longer have to worry about making the right moves to secure promotion, getting recognised and rewarded for my efforts, or even losing my job in the event of a downturn. I have also seen many colleagues follow the same route – some for good, some for a short time to tide them over between full-time posts.

A number of these people asked me for advice on matters ranging from bookkeeping or finding business to working from home and buying equipment. I have always been happy to oblige because, unlike the cut-throat competitiveness of some corporate or agency environments, there is a great camaraderie in the world of freelance copywriting. This is hardly surprising. As I mention in Chapter 1, getting on with people is almost a prerequisite to surviving as an independent copywriter, and it pays to have an informal network among whom to share work if there is a glut. Furthermore, surviving on your own, with nothing but your creativity, writing skill and possibly a few contacts, is a daunting affair to say the least, so talking to people who have done it or are intending to do it can be a great morale booster.

Offering advice and giving confidence to a wider range of people was one of the reasons I decided to write this book. There is another, though, that makes up for the fact that I could be doing myself out of business by passing on the tips of the trade. It is that, even in this age of marketing supremacy, I believe the value of good copy is still understated – and often because copywriters themselves are unable to sell the worth of their work articulately.

The result is that copywriting is often seen as a job anyone can do (true, up to a point) regardless of their experience, talent or training (untrue). Consequently, a lot of marketing copy is badly written, perpetuating the myth that it cannot be worth much. There is a great deal of evidence to show the contrary (which I shall not go into in this book, although some of it can be found in the reference works quoted and much of it, in any case, may be self-evident), but the need for a more professional approach nevertheless remains. In this book I have made a conscious effort to remind copywriters of how they can ensure their work meets consistently high standards and their decisions can be justified according to basic principles of language, grammar and communications effectiveness. I have also indicated where it is worth putting your writing ethics aside and making compromises for the sake of your business relationship with clients; you do, after all, need to make a living.

I therefore hope this book will give existing and would-be copywriters the tools and confidence to strike out on their own and to provide a service which can be shown to yield results for clients, increasing both the perceived value of the writer and that of professionally produced communications in general.

One caution before we go on. While I have had valuable input from a number of sources in compiling this book, it remains predominantly based on my own experience. My way of doing things has worked for me and for my clients over the years, but that does not mean you may necessarily agree with all the points I will make in the pages to follow. That's fine. One great thing about copywriting is that you never stop learning. You pick up new information all the time, which you can either incorporate into your own working methods or discard. If you feel that at least a small part of what I have to say is useful and helpful, then I will consider this work a success. Drop me an email, at the address at the end of this book, and let me know. Let me know also if there are any points you disagree with – and what your own point of view is. I am still learning too, after all.

Jason Deign

Part One
YOUR BUSINESS

1

Why Become a Copywriter?

1. What is copywriting?

Imagine a job where you earn good money for your creativity and your ideas. Where you create wealth from nothing, using just the power of your imagination and a flair for prose. Where you work the hours you want, anywhere you want. Where you choose whom you work for – and how much you get paid.

If this sounds like the kind of work only a musician or novelist could aspire to, think again. Thousands of people enjoy just such a lifestyle – as freelance copywriters, the hired guns that create the commercial messages that make up much of the fabric of our everyday environment.

> **Throughout this book I use the terms 'freelance' and 'independent' interchangeably to indicate someone who runs their own copywriting business.**

Every word in an advert, brochure, leaflet or mail shot has to be written by someone, somewhere. Many more are penned by people who work in publishing – not just for papers and magazines, but also on websites, company newsletters and elsewhere. They, in turn, often rely on information written by public relations agencies and departments.

And virtually every one of these words is paid for. Several thousand people in the UK earn a living from writing commercial material. Some do it in-house, as part of marketing or communications departments within large companies. Some work in advertising, direct mail, new media or public relations agencies. Some do it part-time as part of a wider role. And many ply their trade independently, working where, when, how and for whom they want.

Copywriting, not copyrighting

'Copy' is a term used in the press and advertising industries to mean 'text', so 'copywriting' refers to the business of providing written words for these and other commercial activities. It is not to be confused with 'copyright', which is a legal discipline concerned with the right of an author not to have their work copied without consent and/or payment. Because of the nature of their work, copywriters often need to know a bit about copyright – although not vice versa!

A short history of ad copywriting

The advertising copywriter's trade can be traced back to ancient times, when public criers circulated through the streets calling attention to the sale of items such as slaves and cattle. Advertisements began to appear in the seventeenth century, for products such as coffee (1652) and chocolate (1657). In the early twentieth century, ad agencies, which up till then had simply been brokers for space in newspapers, became involved in producing commercial messages, including copy and art work. Commercial television reached the UK in 1955; the first TV ad in the country was for Gibb's SR toothpaste.

Breaking into the field

Breaking into this field is not as difficult as you might think. Few of those who specialise in copywriting have any formal training. Some, frankly, are not even particularly good. So if you have ever read an advert, brochure or mail shot and thought you could do better, the chances are you could be right – and you could earn good money into the bargain.

Markets

The commercial market for words is massive and it is expanding all the time as new types of media provide new channels for businesses to deliver brand- or sales-related messages. The massive increase in communications brought about by the world wide web, for example, has on its own opened up a wealth of opportunities for writers by creating an environment where news has to be updated every few minutes and company information becomes out of date if it is not renewed every week or so.

This is a far cry from the origins of copywriting, within the advertising industry more than a century ago, when writers paired up with art directors to come up with catchy slogans for the first commercials. Before those days, ads and other promotional messages were usually penned by someone such as the business's proprietor, and, depending on the personality of the author, tended to be full of brash, unsubstantiated claims or, at the other extreme, to read like dry public information notices. By ditching this *ad hoc* approach and carrying out empirical studies on the kinds of messages the public would respond to, the first admen were able to transform the effectiveness of advertising and, it could be argued, help bring about the brand-dominated landscape we live in today.

In the process, much more emphasis was placed on the way words were used and certain rules of thumb, which I will come to later in this book, were developed to improve results. These rules have spread to other areas where the demand for promotional text has grown, such as in direct mail, public relations and the internet. Meanwhile, the news media – radio, TV and, particularly, press – have also for many decades been a major market for writers, albeit one where the demand is for a different form of prose from the sales-oriented text produced by advertising copywriters. However, as I will point out later in this book, producing journalistic copy relies on many of the same principles that govern other forms of copywriting. And in recent years, traditional media owners have increasingly branched out into new areas, such as contract publishing or even internal communications, which are less about hard-nosed investigative reporting and have more in common with manifestly commercial activities such as advertising or public relations.

A competent copywriter today might be expected – and should be able – to turn their hand to any of these areas, regardless of their background.

> **Although it may not be obvious, the chances are that independent copywriters have had a hand in a lot of the commercial messages you see every day. In order to get a job in a big advertising agency, for example, freelance creative teams will often do work experience at greatly reduced rates, just to get a foot in the door. Typically, these teams will be put to work on low-value bread-and-butter print and poster campaigns while the top agency minds are engaged in producing the more lucrative and prestigious cinema and TV commercials. Elsewhere, press, public relations and direct mail agencies, among others, commonly resort to freelancers to supplement their in-house teams.**

Experience and qualifications

Most independent copywriters gain their early experience by working in a relevant post within a company – writing for a publisher, for example, or an advertising agency. For some, going it alone is simply a means of making a living in between jobs; and when it comes to producing words, freelance work can have every bit as much credibility on a CV as full-time employment. While such a path can provide a good grounding and, often, a valuable network of contacts that can be exploited later, a background in writing is by no means a prerequisite to success as an independent copywriter. Nor do you need to have any specific qualifications. Training is available (and I list some sources later in this book) but, again, is not necessary and is really no substitute for on-the-job experience. Most copywriters are self-taught to a large degree in any case. Anyone with a sound knowledge of language and grammar and a flair for writing can make a go of it. And everything you need to know to get started is in this book.

2. The Right Qualities

Nevertheless, there are certain qualities that can help, and might be worth developing. Good copywriters are likely to have many or all of the following.

Listening and questioning skills

As I describe in Chapter 3, the first time you speak to a client to take a brief can often be the most important contact you have with them.

> **The brief is the outline of any piece of work you are asked to do. It can be verbal or written and may involve a face-to-face meeting or just a phone conversation. As with an exam question, you are unlikely to score points if you do not understand it, so it makes sense to clarify as many points as you can. There is more on this in Chapter 3.**

In the short amount of time you may have available – sometimes as little as ten or 15 minutes – you need to understand not only the job the client is asking you to do, but also the audience your work is intended for, the medium that will be used to convey it and, crucially, the cultural nuances of the client's business, to ensure your copy reflects their tone and style accurately. To get this kind of information, you need to be a good listener and ask the right sorts of questions.

The same skills are needed for interviews, which usually form the basis of copy in newsletters, magazines, papers, websites, reports and a host of other communications, and for feedback on your work, which may provide you with essential clues to help you hold on to business.

The client is the person or organisation you work for. (In this book I have followed the industry custom of using 'client' to refer to both indiscriminately.) People who write copy in-house – for example, within an internal communications department – may have clients within the same organisation. But the norm, whether you are working independently or in an agency, is for the client to be employed in a separate business. This means you have to understand their business as well as your own. If you are working for a client on behalf of an agency, you may need to consider two company cultures: that of the client and that of the agency which is paying your wages.

Creativity

Copywriting is generally seen as a highly creative discipline and, while other aspects of the job are perhaps equally important, it is true that good copywriters have to think laterally and possess a good imagination or else they might never get beyond a blank piece of paper. However, if you are going to make a living from copywriting, then creativity needs to be tempered with practicality. Although most clients appreciate good ideas, not all may be receptive to your wackier proposals. And unless you are happy to provide them with something more suitable, you may end up cutting off potentially lucrative sources of income. Good copywriters learn to channel their imagination so their inspiration is couched in terms the client will understand and relate to – in other words, so it fits in with the client's culture.

Beware of ideas above your client's station. Sometimes you can have an idea that you believe is absolutely right for your client – if only they will be prepared to try something a bit riskier than they currently do elsewhere in their communications.

Although you may well be right about the effectiveness of the idea, in practice few clients are bold enough to buy into a concept that goes beyond the boundaries of their corporate culture. So a copywriter who wants to win business will always provide a fall-back idea that, while perhaps less ambitious, fits in with the kind of communication the client is used to seeing.

Attention to detail

Because it rarely seems to go hand-in-hand with creativity, attention to detail is probably the one skill that many prospective (and some practising) copywriters lack. But it is immensely important. The copywriter's job is to produce messages for their client's organisation – and the subliminal content of these messages, the *way* things are said, can be just as important as *what* is said. No matter how creative, copy that is riddled with spelling mistakes or grammatical errors will hardly enhance your client's reputation. If your client notices mistakes, they will be well within their rights to query your abilities – or decide not to use your services again in future. If they do not pick up on errors, then their customers may, and your copy will still fail to achieve its aims.

Remember, as a copywriter you are expected to be an expert in language and writing. Everyone makes mistakes, but dotting 'i's and crossing 't's is probably more essential in copywriting than in any other profession.

Incidentally, this is one area where even journalists, who are specially trained to watch out for inaccuracies in reporting, can come unstuck, because they often learn to dash out words as quickly as possible and rely on editors and sub-editors to pick up on mistakes. The independent copywriter rarely has this luxury, and has to act as both the writer *and* the editor.

Self-motivation

One of the great things about working as a freelance copywriter is that you can do as little or as much work as you want or need to. But no matter how lackadaisical you might be about working, sooner or later you will need to haul yourself out of bed, or away from the TV, to get a job done before the deadline, or to make a few calls so your source of income does not run out completely.

Like being at college, in copywriting you can get by, provided your outgoings are not too high, with relatively little effort. But the more you put in, the more you are likely to get out.

Business acumen

Free spirits might see the ins and outs of running a company as too dull and complicated to be worth worrying about. But while it is true that you do not need much knowledge in this area to run a successful copywriting business, it is important to have some skills at least. Most independent copywriters work alone and have to be adept not only at selling their services, but also at pricing their time properly, keeping on top of invoices and payment and carrying out many other tasks that will ensure a steady income.

This might seem like a fairly straightforward affair, but virtually every copywriter I know of, myself included, has managed to run into cash flow problems at some point, and usually as a result of something simple like not putting aside enough money to cover the tax bill.

Knowing how to run a business may also help you understand some of the challenges faced by your client, which in turn will help you deliver copy that meets their requirements.

An easygoing disposition

Good independent copywriters are often really nice people. They need to be. When a client buys into a copywriter, they are buying a person rather than a product or team. And while ostensibly they are buying a copywriter's writing ability, they will often make a choice on the basis of personality, presentation and so on rather than on the evidence presented in a portfolio. The most important thing for many clients is that the copywriter 'clicks' with them and their business – in other words, that the copywriter can empathise with and understand the client. A copywriter's livelihood is dependent on their ability to meet and get on with a wide range of clients. And their ability to deliver good copy depends on them being sympathetic to the client's needs and circumstances. Copywriters have to be able to accept, with good grace, requests or changes that may go against the grain of what they believe in. Sometimes they have to challenge existing ways of thinking and doing things, without creating ill feeling. Away from clients, independent copywriters often rely on a network of like-minded people for related services such as design or promotion. So if you would rather not deal with people, perhaps you should think about a different kind of business.

How did you score?

This is not a test! If you lack the skills outlined above, this does not necessarily mean copywriting is out of the question. And you need not spend too much time, effort or money to find out.

This book can help you learn the basics so you can try your hand as a copywriter and see if you like it. You could still make money from the experience, even if you do not make a life-long career of it.

3. Running Your Own Business

In any event, if you want to become a freelance copywriter you will also have to consider if you possess the qualities you need to run your own business and work independently. For example:

◆ The freedom to work from home is a big plus for many copywriters but may well not suit someone who really enjoys working as part of a close-knit team, or who shares a cramped living space with other occupants.

◆ Chasing invoices may be OK for those who have no problem focusing on the financial side of business, but for many it is a chore that, no matter how important, is liable to be left to one side.

◆ As with any form of self-employment, there is no cast-iron guarantee of income, which could prove a disincentive for those with major commitments or those who simply appreciate the security of a monthly pay cheque.

There are ways around many of these problems. Partners may be able to help with administration, for example, and people who do not like working alone may find it easier to hire space in a busy office environment. But it pays to give these problems some thought before you embark on a freelance career.

It can also help to talk to friends or work associates who run their own businesses, even if they are in a different field, to find out what pitfalls they have encountered and how they have dealt with them.

Also, think about the times you have had to work on your own, either as part of a job or perhaps while studying for exams. If you found it difficult, the chances are you might face similar problems if you go it alone as an independent copywriter.

Do you have to specialise?

Theoretically there is no reason why a good writer cannot turn their hand to almost any form of prose; witness how many novelists are or were previously journalists, for example. In practice, however, many copywriters choose to specialise to some degree, either because they find it easier to master certain types of writing (direct mail, for instance) or because they develop in-depth knowledge about certain market sectors.

What is it like to be a freelance copywriter?

Copywriting is an ideal way to make money by working for yourself and using your brains and creativity. As your own boss, you can choose when and how much to work, and even who to work for. Since you are unlikely to need to employ other people, the book-keeping and legal aspects of your business will be fairly straightforward. The work can be almost as varied as you want it to be and, if you can demonstrate the value of what you do, charging good money for it should not be a problem. Perhaps the best part of the job, however, is that you get paid exactly for the effort you put in. There can be few feelings more satisfying than the knowledge that each of the carefully-crafted sentences you have put together for a client is earning you pennies and pounds.

A typical day in the life of a copywriter

Freelance copywriting work is so varied that you are unlikely to have the same routine each day. But an average day might involve:

◆ Checking for emails regarding new jobs or work in progress

◆ Taking briefs in person, by phone or email

◆ Replying with time scales and costs

◆ Doing research or background reading

◆ Drafting copy or making changes to an existing draft

◆ Chasing material or approval for a piece of work

◆ Making new business calls

◆ Networking with business contacts

◆ Invoicing or doing other administrative work

◆ Checking finished work.

4. Earnings

The final question you will probably want to take into account when considering your own copywriting business is how much you might expect to earn.

There is no easy answer to this. As with many other types of business, the amount you get out is likely to be largely related to how much you put in. At the highest end of the spectrum, top creative teams in advertising can go on to found their own agencies that, in time, may be worth millions. As an independent copywriter, it is more likely your income will be dictated by how much work you can do on your own, and how much you can charge for your talents.

Copywriting rates vary immensely but even as little as £100 a day can guarantee a salary of more than £20,000 a year, given a steady stream of work. Good practitioners can easily expect to earn up to two or three times this amount. In addition, those who work from home will be able to write off part of their household expenses against tax, so they will effectively keep more of the money they earn than their counterparts in full-time employment.

However, unless you have a ready-made network of contacts, or a client that can guarantee regular, well-paid work, it is wise to assume that it may take a few months to build up a good income. Here, though, copywriting offers a better deal than many other business start-ups in that the initial outlay needed is fairly minimal. And, as with other businesses, Her Majesty's Revenue and Customs provides a further break by not asking for tax until up to 18 months from the time you start trading – although that does not mean it is not a good idea to put some money aside to allow for it.

For many people, the move into freelance copywriting is a lifestyle decision rather than a financial one. There can be few other jobs that offer such freedom, variety and satisfaction.

International earning potential

One of the great things about copywriting is that you can work for people anywhere in the world, no matter where you are based. In Chapter 8 I provide guidelines on how to adapt copy for foreign audiences and clients. Touting your talents abroad also involves thinking about the way you promote and price your services – both covered in Chapter 6.

> **If you have read this far and feel freelance copywriting is the thing for you, then congratulations. Stick with me through the rest of this book and before long you should know enough to get started. I hope you will enjoy making your livelihood in copywriting as much as I do, and find it rewarding in other ways, too.**

2

Getting Started

1. The Good News

So you have decided to set up your own business as a copywriter. Quite apart from worries about how your technical abilities will measure up when you go it alone, you are likely to be daunted by the prospect of having to handle the business side of your enterprise and sorting out all those complex areas, such as tax, invoicing, promotion or legal matters, that are usually 'someone else's department' in the cosy world of employment. Indeed, it is probably the fears about having to operate a business, rather than doubts about one's abilities as a copywriter, which put most people off setting up independently.

Well, here are three bits of good news.

♦ First, while there is a certain amount of red tape and administration involved in setting up a business, it is far from excessive; certainly not enough to deter the thousands of people, from plumbers and cab drivers to lawyers and architects, who do start and run their own businesses successfully every year.

♦ Second, you do not have to deal with that much on day one. As a copywriter, you can start trading with just a few bare essentials and incorporate most of the trappings of your business, such as stationery, detailed accounts and even much of your equipment, in the weeks or months that follow. The government requires you to register for things like taxation, but it recognises that the main priority for new businesses is to start earning money, so it imposes relatively few requirements on you at the outset and usually allows many aspects of your business dealings to be backdated.

♦ Third, the effort you have to put into administration is compensated for by the fact that running your own business offers many benefits which simply are not available to employees. Quite apart from improving your lifestyle – no commuting to the office or working overtime without pay, for example – being able to offset many of your expenses against tax means the taxman ends up with less of your cash.

> **Nevertheless, there will probably be a few things you want to get straight in your mind before you take the plunge. Like, for example, when you should do it.**

2. The Basics

When is the best time to start?

Not everyone gets to choose when they can set up a business. For many copywriters, self-employment may come unexpectedly as a result of redundancy or in response to an unforeseen change in circumstances. Otherwise, the timing might be dictated by the end of a course of study or other change in professional circumstances. In some cases, though, you might have the luxury of picking your moment, and you might be wondering when is best.

The short answer is that you can set up your business at any time, but it helps to be assured of some work from the outset.

Preferably, you should have a good idea of how much you need or want to earn (see 'Having a business plan', below) and firm offers of regular work that will cover most of your required income.

You can usually count on picking up extra clients once you get going, but remember that not every promise of a job results in an assignment. For the same reason, be wary of setting up in business on the basis of a single project, no matter how large, unless you are reasonably confident you can sell your skills elsewhere too.

If you are in full-time employment, you might want to work out your full notice to give you time to start thinking about and working on your business. It also helps to leave on good terms – your former employer may well turn out to be a valued client.

In any event you should, if you can, start lining up work a good few weeks in advance of your proposed start date. In the fortnight or so leading up to D-day, warm up your contacts and get firm briefs or contracts.

It is all very well to 'open up shop' and hope for trade to come rolling through the door, but copywriting is not like owning a shop. You have to go out and get the business. And there is no better way to start than to have a project in hand.

Who will be involved in your business?

Most independent copywriters set up in business on their own. After all, what they are selling are their own, particular skills. However, there might be reasons why you would want to go into business with others.

◆ You may know someone whose skills are a good fit with yours, either as a copywriter or in an allied field such as design or marketing. Going into business together might improve your chances of success because you will be able to cross-sell each other's services. But bear in mind that finding two salaries may be more than twice as difficult as finding one. If you are unsure about whether the partnership will work, it could be a good idea to first try forming an informal alliance, trading separately and independently but taking on projects together.

◆ If you are fortunate enough to be certain of a guaranteed high level of business, you might feel you will need to employ other copywriters and staff to do other work, such as running your accounts. In this case, you will probably want to talk to a business adviser about putting together a detailed business plan (see below) and perhaps doing some research to make doubly sure of your profit expectations before setting out.

◆ If you have a partner who is not in full-time employment, there can be tax advantages to their being involved in your business. Paying a member of your family to help out with things such as administration can count as a tax-deductible expense for your business, for example, and cut your costs by using up their personal tax allowance.

Having a business plan

Starting a copywriting business does not usually demand a fully-fledged business plan. After all, you are not likely to need to sell your idea to anyone, unless you need to approach your bank for a loan for equipment. However, it is definitely advisable to put your ideas about your business in order and make a few calculations to be sure it will be viable. Things you need to consider include:

◆ Roughly how much do you need or want to earn a year?

◆ How many days a year can you realistically expect to work? (Remember to subtract holidays and weekends – and do not expect to get work five days a week, every week.)

◆ Your expected earnings divided by the days you work will give you an idea of the minimum day rate you need to charge. Now ask yourself whether it is realistic. (See Chapter 6 for more on pricing.)

◆ Where will you find the clients to provide you with this work? (Again, see Chapter 6 for more on this, but you should preferably have a good idea of where your clients will come from before you get started.)

◆ Have you taken into account the costs of setting up your business – buying equipment and so on – plus other outgoings, such as office space (if you intend to rent it)?

Whether or not you formalise these points on paper is up to you, but it will definitely help build your confidence and probably improve your chances of success if you go through the exercise. It can also help to set goals for your business – increasing your turnover by a certain amount each year, for

form of a dividend, increasing the amount of cash you can keep if you are a higher-rate taxpayer. Also, if the business runs into trouble, the liability for losses is limited to the company (hence the name 'limited company') and although directors do have a measure of personal responsibility for the affairs of the business, they are not exposed to the level of risk that they would be as sole traders or partners. However, there is a downside. Establishing a limited company involves more administration. Accounts and annual returns have to be filed at Companies House every year within specified dates, for example, and it is essential to appoint a company secretary and follow established procedures in the running of the business. As a director, you will be an employee of the company and will be subject to benefit-in-kind rules which will mean you will incur additional tax and National Insurance for things like company cars.

Failure to comply with these requirements can be a criminal offence.

Which is best?

There are no hard and fast rules as to which type of business you should set up. You will need to consider which best suits the kind of operation you have in mind. For example:

◆ If you do not anticipate earning enough to put you in the higher-rate tax bracket (around £34,600 a year) and shudder at the thought of a lot of paperwork, you would probably be better off working as a sole trader.

◆ If your earnings are likely to exceed £34,000 and you have a spouse or partner who is earning less, forming a partnership can allow you to split the profits from your business so you do not end up paying higher rate tax.

◆ A limited company can appear more professional and, potentially, is a good option if you are planning to go into business with others. But it involves a degree more hassle and is unlikely to be worth the effort unless you plan to earn substantial amounts of money.

Of course, there is nothing to stop you starting out with one type of business and altering it as your circumstances change. However, bear in mind that moving up the scale from sole trader to partnership to limited company is a lot more straightforward than doing the reverse.

> **For its simplicity, the sole trader arrangement makes a good starting point. If you are not sure, though, it makes sense to speak to a business adviser or an accountant.**

4. Other Considerations

What about VAT?

If your turnover is more than £64,000 in a 12-month period (at the time of writing – check with your local Revenue and Customs office or accountant to see if this is still the current level), you have to register with Her Majesty's Revenue and Customs for Value Added Tax (VAT) and add a charge of 17.5 per cent to your bills. Below £64,000, you can register for VAT if you want to. Being VAT-registered will entitle you to claim back VAT on your expenses (more on this in Chapter 5) and can give the impression of a bigger business, but you will have to file VAT returns every quarter. Also note that certain clients, such as those involved in insurance, education or transport, are not able to reclaim VAT, so, for them, registering would effectively make your fees higher than those of non-registered competitors.

You will probably want to weigh up whether the size and status of your business will warrant the extra effort you will have to put into being VAT-registered. In any case, you should keep an eye on your turnover once it starts to creep up towards £64,000 in a 12-month period as there are penalties for not registering when you reach this limit.

In my experience, it makes little difference to clients whether you are VAT registered or not. So if you do not expect to have a high turnover, you might be better off not registering and saving yourself the hassle of having to prepare VAT returns every three months.

In any case, registering for VAT once you are up and running is a very straightforward affair. Although it does involve more work, and there are penalties and interest charged on unpaid VAT if you miss filing deadlines, you might find that preparing your accounts every quarter helps you keep better track of how well your business is doing.

Also beware that the threshold for VAT is on turnover, not profit, so you may have to register in any case if you are handling large-value jobs, such as print work, that you recharge directly to your client(s).

Naming your business

Since you will effectively be selling yourself and your skills, there is no need to come up with a fancy name for your business. Your own name should be the one you promote. The exception to this might be if you feel it is important to emphasise that more than one person is involved in the business, for example if you decide to set up a partnership or a limited company. In the first case, you might want to reflect the nature of your business in its name: 'Joe Bloggs Partners' or 'Joe Bloggs Partnership' for instance. Another option might be 'Joe Bloggs Associates'. If you have a limited company, you might want to get away altogether from any association with your own name, although you cannot set up a limited company with the same name as someone else in your line of business. You might also find there are few word combinations that can usefully and meaningfully be applied to your company and which have not been taken already.

A further consideration is whether or to what extent you want to promote your business over the internet. You will probably want to check whether the name you want to trade with has not already been registered on the internet by someone else.

If you have a website, its *domain name* is a unique method of identification by which people can find it, a bit like a postal address. Like postal addresses, you cannot use one that has already been taken; and following the explosion of internet services in the late 90s, many have.

You can find this out easily through any number of domain name registration services. Your internet service provider (ISP) will probably provide a domain name look-up feature on its home page; otherwise, you could try www.netnames.com. For more on promoting your service online, see Chapter 6.

Stationery

While you are working out what to call yourself, you may well start wondering whether you need to get professionally designed and printed business cards and stationery. These things can all help you project a more professional image and business cards, at least, can be useful in helping you get your name and contact details about. They are not an essential prerequisite for your business, however.

> **If you can get them done well and cheaply, then go ahead, but otherwise my advice would be to concentrate on getting your first commissions rather than worrying too much about the look of your stationery.**

When you do get round to designing your stationery, either on your own computer or with professional help, make sure you remember to include all your contact details: address, phone and, if you have them, fax, mobile, email and website. Also, if you are relying on your own design skills, try not to get too carried away with fancy typefaces or desk-top publishing effects unless you are a reasonably able designer. You will get a more professional look with a plain, understated layout.

Getting your priorities right

There is an argument to say the first thing you need to worry about when you set up your business is not the business itself, but making a profit; selling your skills, getting commissions and completing work quickly so you can invoice your clients and be assured of money flowing into your shiny new coffers.

This is undoubtedly true and some aspects of setting up a business make it easier to concentrate on profits. Income tax, for example, does not need to be paid until well over a year after you have got started. But, clearly, ignoring your tax affairs for this amount of time is hardly a recipe for success.

> **Luckily, even with a lot of work to do, you should be able to find pockets of spare time in the initial stages to enable you to take care of the administrative side of running your business.**

5. What You Absolutely Have To Do

The one thing you have to do when you start up business is to let the tax authorities know. If you are working freelance, clients might need to see evidence of your self-employed status before they take you on, so they can be sure they will not be held liable for your National Insurance contributions.

If you are setting up as a sole trader, you will need to notify your local tax office in order to get a Schedule D number. To find out more, contact your local tax office. They are listed in the phone book and they will also tell you how to pay Class 2 National Insurance Contributions.

◆ Your tax office can also advise you on what to do if you set up a partnership.

◆ If you are setting up a company, you will need to notify Companies House. You can find out more from the Companies House website, www.companieshouse.co.uk.

◆ If you expect to earn more than around £64,000 a year, you will need to register for VAT. You do this with Her Majesty's Revenue and Customs. Again, details of your nearest office can be found in the phone book, under 'VAT'.

Unless you want to do your own accounts, you might also want to appoint an accountant for your business. You will not need them to do any work at the beginning, but they can provide valuable help and advice on starting out. To find an accountant, ask other self-employed people or small businesses for recommendations, if possible. Otherwise, you could look for someone local in the *Yellow Pages.*

You might want to speak to a few prospective advisers before you choose one. Ask for a written quote of their rates. These can vary widely, but should not really be more than a few hundred pounds for the preparation of one year's accounts and a tax return, if you have got good bookkeeping records. Also, check to see if they have experience in your area of business.

You may be relying on your accountant to represent your business to the tax authorities, so it will help if they have a good understanding of what you do so they can argue your case most effectively.

3

Getting Kitted Out

1. What You Need To Get Going

One of the great things about setting up a copywriting business is how little outlay you need to make to get going.

At its simplest, you can get away with a phone, a personal computer (PC) or Apple Macintosh with a standard word processor such as Microsoft Word, plus a printer, email and internet access – all of which can be bought cheaply as a bundle, and the costs of which you could probably recoup with your first commission. You might not even have to worry about such basic equipment if your first few jobs are on client premises.

On top of that, you may find it useful to have a fax machine (unless your computer has software which allows it to send and receive faxes) and, quite possibly, other equipment such as a dictaphone or tape recorder, a scanner (particularly if you intend to have your own website) and something to back up your work on.

Nowadays, you should be able to pick up pretty much all of this for less than £1,000. Also, bear in mind that most of the technology covered in this chapter is affected by Moore's Law (after Gordon Moore, the founder of Intel), which basically says that the amount of computer memory available per dollar doubles every 18 months. This helps drive down prices for everything from laptops to printers at a fairly steady rate, so be aware that some of the prices quoted here may go quickly out of date.

You may also need to buy shelves, a desk and a chair if you do not have furniture to hand that you can use in your office. Again, however, this is unlikely to set you back more than a few hundred pounds.

Remember that you do not need to shell out for a complete, high-tech office environment from the outset. It may well be best to buy the absolute minimum you need and add or upgrade your office furniture and equipment when you need to or have some spare cash to afford it.

Keep the receipts for everything you buy as these expenses are all tax-deductible.

2. Your Computer

Your computer will be your primary business tool and it is worth taking some time to make the right decision when choosing it, if you do not already have one. The options available can seem a little daunting, but things you will need to consider include:

New or second-hand?

If you are really strapped for cash, you might want to consider buying a computer second-hand. Before you do, however, bear in mind the following:

◆ Computers double in power and halve in price roughly every 18 months (see Moore's Law above), so even a new computer bought today will probably be obsolete in a few years' time. A second-hand model will have even less useful life left.

◆ For the same reason, the speed, memory and software of any second-hand computers are likely to be significantly inferior to those of a new model.

◆ Many manufacturers (Dell, for example) will allow you to customise your computer when you buy it new, so you pay only for the things you need. With a second-hand computer you get what you see, and the price might be bumped up by a flashy games card or suchlike that will be of no use to you in your business.

My advice would be to buy a new computer if you do not have one already. You can keep the price down by shopping around and selecting only the features you need.

PC or Apple Mac?

A few years ago the choice of whether to buy a PC or an Apple Macintosh would have been a major one for most budding copywriters. The trendy Apple has always been the favoured tool of creative industries such as design and publishing, largely because it is easy to use and its operating system is geared towards handling graphics files and the like. PCs, on the other hand, have become the main platform in most other businesses because they are cheaper and perfectly competent at handling most corporate applications.

As a result, many creative software applications, like QuarkXPress, the professional desktop publishing package used by most publishers, were initially developed with the Apple in mind, while general business applications like the Microsoft Office suite of products (which includes Word, the most widely used word processor) were designed for the PC. For a long time, too, both types of computer had great difficulty understanding each other, so you needed special programs to make Apple files readable on a PC and vice versa.

These days, however, PC and Apple systems are largely interoperable and most common software works on both, so which one you choose is largely a matter of personal taste. Writing generally looks smaller on Apple Mac screens than on a PC. And Apple Macs have other quirks (such as no right-click mouse button) which can take a bit of getting used to if you have worked with PCs before. Apples are, however, undeniably better looking, easier to use and generally faster and more responsive than PCs.

> **If you are really not sure which type of computer to choose, you might want to think about where the bulk of your work will come from. If your clients are likely to be ad agencies or publishing houses, it would make sense to buy an Apple Mac as this is the type of computer they are most likely to use. If you expect most of your projects to be for corporate clients, then a PC might be a safer bet.**

Desktop versus laptop

Another question is whether it is worth investing in a laptop computer instead of a bulkier desktop. Again, this is largely a question of personal taste. Points that might influence your decision include:

◆ Laptops tend to be about a third more expensive than desktops but this extra expense might be worth it if you do not have much space in your office or will gain extra work from being able to carry your computer with you.

◆ If you do buy a laptop and intend to carry it around a lot, you will probably want to take out extra insurance to cover accidental damage, loss or theft. Remember to back up your work often.

◆ Laptops can be more prone to wear and tear than desktops, and more difficult and expensive to upgrade.

◆ However, a portable computer can be very useful if you are likely to need to make presentations to existing or prospective clients.

If you think a laptop would be useful, points to consider when making your purchase include:

◆ **Screen size, brightness and resolution.** If your laptop is going to stay in your office most of the time, it makes sense to go for the largest and highest-resolution screen possible, for the sake of your eyes. Also bear in mind that dim screens can be impossible to see in bright light.

◆ **Peripherals and connectors.** As with all computers, try to make sure your laptop is as 'connectable' as possible. You might also want to find out if your laptop can connect to the internet via your mobile phone, or link to other computers via a network.

◆ **Size and weight.** While a larger laptop might not be a bad buy (because you will have a better sized screen and keyboard to work with), if you are going to take it out with you, you will want it to be as light as possible.

◆ **Battery life.** The longer the better, if you intend to do a lot of work while travelling. If you regularly face long journeys it may be worth buying a spare battery to take with you.

If you intend to carry the laptop around a lot, you will probably want to buy a sturdy carry case, too.

3. Software

Software usually comes bundled with your computer and in some cases you can save a few pennies by buying a machine that is filled with programs from lesser-known vendors. This may well prove to be a false economy. Like it or not, the world and its dog all use Microsoft Office products and if you do not then you are bound to get stuck sooner or later when a client sends you an extremely important Excel spreadsheet or PowerPoint presentation that you cannot read.

It is also not a good idea to assume you will be able to pick up a bootleg or cheap copy of whatever you need later on. First, bootlegs are illegal and your lawyer (if you have one) would probably recommend that you stay on the right side of the law if you want to run a successful business. Second, even discounted versions of stand-alone programs such as PowerPoint or Excel could set you back hundreds of pounds – more than it would cost you to buy the whole lot as a bundle when you first purchase your computer.

When you are looking at software, I would recommend you get Microsoft Word, PowerPoint and Excel as a bare minimum, if for no other reason than your clients are likely to send you files in these formats. Outlook and

Internet Explorer – Microsoft's email and internet browser programs – will come as standard with any Office package.

> In general, most of the software you will need to deal with files over the internet can be downloaded for free or for a small fee, which is tax-deductible.

Word processors, browsers and email

The three most important pieces of software you will use as a copywriter are a word processor (for writing), a web browser (for internet access) and email (for communicating with clients and contacts). Unless you have bought a computer from another planet, the chances are you will get all three bundled with your machine. If you are using a PC then you will end up using Microsoft Word and Microsoft Internet Explorer. If you buy an Apple, you will get Pages (which is compatible with Word) and Safari. Either way, you will be ready to go.

You will also, as likely as not, get either Microsoft Outlook or Mail, depending on whether you are using a PC or a Mac. Both will be fine, although when it comes to email you might want to remember that there is a wide range of options to choose from and you may want to take advantage of more than one. A webmail account, using a provider such as Hotmail, Yahoo! or Gmail, can be handy as a backup where you need to provide an email address but are wary of being spammed, or will need to access emails frequently while on the move. Another email system commonly found in large businesses is Lotus Notes from IBM, which is used by more than 120 million people worldwide, although you are unlikely to encounter it unless you are working for a client that uses it.

> Beware that web mail services tend to be less versatile than standard email packages like Outlook Express. And because they are based on independently-hosted websites, they are prone to service breakdowns on occasion.

Security software

In this day and age, some form of software to prevent virus attacks should be viewed as a necessity rather than a luxury. Virus protection packages now come as standard with most computers and can be updated automatically over the internet; with new types of virus appearing almost on a daily basis, if a virus protection system is not frequently updated it soon becomes obsolete.

If your computer does not have a pre-installed virus protection system, you will probably need to pay an annual subscription and download one from the internet. The few pounds it will cost you a year is more than worth the investment.

At best, a virus attack is likely to hamper your work and could prove embarrassing if the virus is transmitted to clients. At worst, some viruses can wipe your computer's hard drive or cripple the machine.

There is little to choose from between virus protection systems. The major suppliers, including McAfee or Sophos, are more or less on a par in terms of their effectiveness (in fact some of them are different brand names for the same companies), so you might as well choose them on the basis of price or recommendation from friends.

One thing that I have discovered, however, is that some of these systems can themselves interfere with the working of your computer and slow it down. If this happens, you will need to remove the program (using the 'uninstall' option within the 'Add/Remove Programs' file in the Control Panel folder of your computer, if you are using Microsoft Office) and try with a different vendor.

If your work is likely to involve handling or generating confidential material, you might want to consider installing a firewall, which acts like an electronic gatekeeper on your computer to prevent hackers from accessing it over the internet; if nothing else, it can help put your clients' minds at ease. One will probably be bundled with your anti-virus system, but if not then a simple, effective and free firewall called Zone Alarm can be downloaded from www.zonealarm.com.

Choosing an Apple Mac computer can help prevent virus attacks as most viruses are designed to infect PCs. It is still wise to get some form of protection for your Macintosh, however.

4. Internet Access

Being able to get online, for internet access, email and other applications, is practically essential in today's business environment. As a copywriter, it is one of the few things I recommend you do not cut corners on. At the time of writing, you can still find internet service providers (ISPs) who will get you online for nothing or next to nothing with a dial-up service, which essentially means making a phone call to connect to your ISP. This will tie up your phone line (unless you have a second line in your workspace) and will not do your phone bill any favours. Also, you might be limited by the speed of the connection.

A far better bet is broadband, which gives you a high-speed, 'always on' connection and leaves your phone line free. Broadband is now available virtually everywhere and the cost is falling rapidly. In any case, the increase in productivity you will get from using it will easily repay your monthly subscription charge.

A broadband connection will also allow you to take the fullest advantage of a number of useful internet applications, such as:

◆ **Voice over IP (VoIP)** services such as Skype. These let you call other users of the same service for free and give you the option of making international calls at greatly reduced rates. VoIP is more than just a phone service, as it incorporates applications ranging from Instant Messaging (see below) to videoconferencing.

◆ **Instant Messaging (IM).** If you work regularly with the same group of clients and contacts then I would strongly urge you to find out if they use IM services such as Windows Live Messenger or Yahoo! Messenger.

These will let you see when people are online and chat to them over the web in real time. This can be useful when you are working closely with them on a project, as messaging is less intrusive than a phone call and quicker (and less formal) then email.

◆ **Social networking sites.** Although there is some debate over the value of sites such as Facebook or MySpace for business, they can serve as a way of keeping in touch with clients and contacts and give you a way of easily showing off your portfolio of work online, if you do not have the time or inclination to put together a website (see Chapter 6).

If you are a laptop user, you might also want to consider installing a wireless network in your workspace. The advantage of this is that it allows you to be a lot more flexible about where you work (you can check emails while eating breakfast in the kitchen, for example) and other people (family members, flatmates or, in a more professional setup, clients and work collaborators) can share your broadband connection. The main technologies to choose from are WiFi and WiMAX. The former, which is traditionally used for home and small office wireless installations, is perfectly good for anything the typical copywriter is likely to need. Obviously, if you are working on client premises or in leased or serviced offices (see next chapter) then the way you get online is likely to be dictated by the type of connectivity provided in the building.

If you travel a lot then you may want to look into getting a mobile data card to plug into your laptop. That way you can get online from anywhere, using the mobile phone network.

The pricing and quality of internet services varies almost from day to day. Before making your final decision of provider, buy a specialist magazine such as *Internet* to get up to speed on the latest offers and recommendations.

5. Computer Peripherals

Printers

Apart from your phone and computer, a printer is likely to be one of your most important technology purchases. You can choose between inkjet or laserjet models. The former are cheaper, but have higher running costs and are probably less cost-effective if you expect to print out large amounts of text.

Another choice is between a black-and-white and a colour machine. Not only are colour printers more expensive than black-and-white ones, but their running costs are higher as well. Colour can help with presentation but is probably only really necessary if your work will include an element of design or layout, for example if you need to provide colour proofs for sign-off.

> **If you are buying a new computer, you may be able to get a printer bundled in with it. Check the printer's list price, but it is likely that the combined price will represent a significant saving.**

Scanners

A scanner is not essential for copywriting, but, again, can be useful if offered at a discount as part of a package when you buy your computer. The main uses for scanners are to incorporate images into documents and websites, and, in conjunction with optical character recognition programs, to scan printed documents directly into word processors so the text can be manipulated. However, with the increasing use of digital images and soft copy (electronic versions of text that can be transferred over the internet) both of these applications are becoming less critical. If needed, a good scanner and its associated software can be picked up at any high street computer store for under £100.

Storage devices

Sooner or later, your computer is going to die. It is a fact of life. And if you have not been saving your work elsewhere on a regular basis, then you (and your clients) will be sorry. Luckily, though, all you need nowadays to make sure that does not happen is a USB flash drive or JumpDrive, available cheaply online or from any computer or electronics store. In fact, you may not even need to buy a flash drive. I currently back up more than a decade's worth of work onto my iPod, which still has plenty of spare space for music, and if you are starting out then you could probably back up your work on your mobile phone. Being able to carry a full set of files around with you like this is particularly handy if you need to access them while away from base, for instance if you are doing some work at a client's premises on their computers, but you may want to consider password-protecting access to sensitive files in case you lose the storage device.

Remember to keep your backup files in a safe place.

Having a good backup system is pointless unless you use it. You should get into the habit of copying your files to disk on a regular basis; monthly at least, and preferably every week.

Other peripherals

It is unlikely you will need anything more than a computer and printer to start with. But as time goes by you could well end up picking up other add-ons, such as a digital camera (which will allow you to download photographs direct to your computer) or cards and connectors that will let you hook your laptop (if you have one) to your mobile (so you can access the internet while travelling). The list of gadgets is almost endless and going into detail about them is beyond the scope of this book.

The only point I would make is that it would probably be unwise to spend your money on anything that cannot help you produce an obvious return. If you do have to buy a new piece of equipment, shop around.

6. Other Equipment

Phones and answer-phones

A phone is probably the most important tool for your business. If you are working from home, it is worth considering a second phone line for work. You can get the phone itself for next to nothing, but since you will be using it a lot you might want to get one that has features such as one-touch memory keys for numbers you call frequently. An answer-phone is also a good idea, although most phone companies (including BT) offer cheap or free network-based voicemail services you can use if necessary.

> **Perhaps the best idea for starters is to buy a combined phone, answering machine and fax (see below), which should not set you back more than about £100.**

Fax machines

Despite the rise of email as the main way of exchanging information between locations, a fax machine is still a useful piece of kit for your business, if only because some clients have automated accounting systems that are programmed to send purchase orders, remittance advices and other types of confirmation by facsimile. However, unless you suspect you will be using the fax a lot, there is probably little reason, initially, to worry about spending too much on this equipment. After more than a decade in business as a freelance copywriter, I still have no problems making do with a machine that shares my phone line and has a built-in answering system for when I am not in.

Mobile phones

If you are one of the few remaining people in the world who does not have a mobile phone, now is probably the time to take the plunge. A mobile is obviously particularly useful if you expect to be away from base a lot, for example working on client premises. Since a missed call can mean missed work, you should keep your mobile with you, and on, as much as possible.

For the same reason, it is preferable to have a regular rather than pay-as-you-go tariff (remember that business phone calls are tax-deductible), so that you do not end up running out of credit in the middle of an important conversation. Take out insurance so you can get a replacement easily if your phone is lost or stolen.

> **Remember to advertise your mobile number on your stationery and promotional material. If you have an answer-phone, make sure you mention your mobile number on the outgoing message.**

Photocopiers

Whether you buy or rent it, a photocopier is an expensive piece of equipment. It is probably not worth investing in unless you will be sharing it (and the cost) with others, or have good reason to expect that you will need to make several copies of documents on a regular basis, or can somehow recoup the cost through the work you do.

- Bear in mind that you can make occasional copies using a fax machine (see above).

- Unless you live somewhere really remote, there is likely to be a copy shop nearby for occasional photocopying jobs. Check your *Yellow Pages* for the nearest.

- Most printers can double up as copiers (and vice versa).

- If you want to buy a photocopier, a second-hand machine is likely to be a great deal cheaper and might still come with a service guarantee.

Dictaphones and digital recorders

A dictaphone or digital recorder is a useful gadget to have to hand for important interviews but I would caution against using one in place of handwritten notes or shorthand.

Trying to track down half a dozen quotable sentences in an hour's worth of recording is a time-consuming process and one that is hardly going to improve your efficiency. Besides, unless you take up investigative reporting you are unlikely to come across situations where you cannot double check facts, figures and phrases later on.

> **If you decide to purchase a recorder, I would advise buying a model which takes standard batteries so you can get hold of new ones easily in an emergency.**

7. Furniture

Wherever you are working, try to make sure your environment is comfortable, safe and healthy. If you are furnishing your workspace yourself, you will probably want to get:

◆ a desk that is large enough to spread your work out on and accommodate your computer, phone and other equipment

◆ a good chair that provides back support and is the right height for your desk

◆ good lighting from an anglepoise desk lamp or similar

◆ shelves or filing cabinets, within easy reach of your workspace.

You do not need to spend a fortune on all this. But make sure you get furniture that is practical and ergonomic, as you will be in close contact with it for some time. Also, it is a good idea to have a sofa or comfy chair in or near your workspace, which you can use to take a break from your computer if, for example, you are reviewing source material or searching for inspiration. (It is a very bad idea to have a TV in front of the sofa or comfy chair.)

There is more on working environments in the next chapter.

8. Vehicles

You do not need a car or other vehicle to be a copywriter but if you have one it can be handy for work-related travel. You can count the cost of business mileage against tax; more of this in Chapter 5. Also, be aware that any travel above and beyond going to and from your place of work could affect your insurance premium – check with your insurer.

4

Where to Work

1. Your Options

A major attraction of running your own copywriting business is that it frees you from having to commute to and from an employer's office every day. Of course, some people relish being in an office environment, which can be an important issue to consider if you are planning to set up on your own. There are three obvious choices of workplace that you will probably be contemplating, which are not necessarily mutually exclusive:

♦ working from home

♦ renting or buying an office

♦ working on client premises.

2. Working From Home

Working from home is the cheapest and easiest option when starting your business but there is a number of important considerations to weigh up before you decide it is the one for you.

♦ Is there enough space to accommodate you and your work equipment without interfering with the living space used by other occupants?

♦ Will other members of the household distract you while you are working?

♦ Will you have adequate and uninterrupted access to phone lines, power points and so on?

Ideally, you will want to have a separate room, away from the passage and noise of other occupants (including pets), which you can use as your office.

A basement or a loft would be a good choice, as would a disused garage, outhouse or shed, provided the space is dry, warm and secure.

Make sure your chosen office area has plenty of headroom, good light, power sockets and so on. You may well want to install a separate phone line or two, for your answer-phone and fax.

> **If you cannot have a room to yourself, try to make sure your work space is in a quiet corner of one that is not used during the day. That space under the stairs might seem like a good spot to put your desk, but how will you cope with people traipsing back and forth behind you?**

Mixing work with family life

Unless you live alone, when working from home you will have to consider the impact other members of your household will have on your business and vice versa. If the other occupants are away during the day you should have less to worry about. But what if you have to work late? And will they mind you working when they have a day off?

Working at home requires serious discipline, both for you and for other members of the household. Just as you will need to resist the temptation to extend your breakfast or lunch break with some 'research' in front of the telly, so you will need to stress to others that you cannot be disturbed when working.

This can be incredibly difficult. Some people refuse to believe that work can happen outside an office and, no matter how busy you are, will gravitate towards you with cups of tea and requests for 'a quick chat' that can end up robbing you of precious time.

Rebuffing such approaches can put a strain on relationships; you will need to learn how to handle situations diplomatically so you can make it clear when you cannot be disturbed without causing offence.

Some home workers get round the problem by adopting a closed-door policy or similar ploy to indicate that they cannot be interrupted. Others have an 'off-limits' rule during given hours of the day. It can be worth talking to people you know who work from home to find out how they cope.

These issues are not just about the effects other people will have on your business. Studies by BT, the telecommunications company, on 'remote working' (in other words, working away from an employer's office) have shown that while people who work from home usually have an increased quality of life, the quality of life of their partners can suffer.

Much of this is because it is easy for home workers to end up doing overtime, eating into what other members of the family consider 'rest time'. This is something you may need to weigh up when considering where to work.

Dealing with interruptions

No matter how well you manage to separate your home–office environment from the rest of your home, there will always be occasions when you have to deal with unexpected interruptions. Here are a few tips on what to do:

◆ In the first place, if you definitely need uninterrupted peace and quiet for a particular length of time, for example to take an important call, it is worth warning other members of the household beforehand.

◆ If you need to take a break from your work, save any documents that you are working on at your computer, even if you expect to be away for only a moment or two. (In fact, it is a good habit to save your work at regular intervals anyway, perhaps at every paragraph or two in the case of important documents, as computer crashes have a nasty habit of coming unannounced.)

◆ Also make a note of the time, if you are charging clients on an hourly or day-rate basis.

◆ If you are in the middle of an important train of thought or piece of research, it is a good idea to jot down a few notes to help you pick up where you left off when you get back.

◆ Keep an eye on how long your break lasts and bear in mind any time-sensitive projects you might have in hand.

You are your own boss, so how you organise your time is up to you. If you need to make time during the day to cope with household commitments, for example because you have a family, you can catch up with work later on, or even decide to cut down the amount of work you take on. However, if you are to provide a professional service then you will need to make sure that outside influences do not stop you from meeting clients' deadlines in good time.

> **If you find 'occasional interruptions' are eating into your work time, you may need to alter the ground rules you have established with other members of the household, or change the way you work.**

Providing a professional image

One constraint of using your home as your office is that it is not likely to be an ideal place in which to hold meetings with clients. This should not usually present a problem. Most clients will be more than happy to see you on their own premises (after all, it saves them travelling). Failing that, a pub or restaurant can be a good place for informal meetings.

If you really need to impress a client, for example in a pitch for a large project, you might want to consider hiring a meeting room in a hotel or suchlike (here again, however, visiting your client's offices is likely to a better idea).

Providing a serious, professional front extends to areas like background noise during phone calls. Quiet music might be acceptable; the sound of a television is unlikely to inspire confidence (and in any case is likely to impair your ability to listen to the caller). With unavoidable background noise (such as the kind my children often create when I am on the phone), the only solution may be to come clean and explain that you are working from home.

Financial and legal considerations

If you work from home then you are entitled to offset a proportion of your household costs, such as electricity and heating, against tax. The taxman will accept an estimate of the amount of energy costs which can be attributed to your work.

So, for example, if you have four rooms in your house (excluding bathrooms, closets and so on) and use one for work, you could claim a quarter of your gas and electricity bills against tax. The same goes for your telephone bill, if your phone is used for business and personal calls. Be sure not to over-claim, however; your accountant will be able to advise on what proportion of costs is likely to be acceptable. (For more on this, see the next chapter.)

On the legal side, it is wise to make sure that your working from home does not invalidate any insurances or tenancy or mortgage agreements.

Provided they are notified, most insurers, landlords and lenders are unlikely to have a problem with you working from home, as long as you make it clear you will not be receiving customers on the premises. In some cases, your insurance premiums might even go down because you can claim to be at home all day.

3. Working in an Office

If you are unable or prefer not to work from home, for example because you are going into business with others, then you will probably need to rent or buy some form of office space. Since buying an office outright is probably beyond the means of most budding copywriters, I shall just concentrate here on the rental options, which are as follows . . .

Leasing space

Leasing office space is a relatively straightforward affair but can be quite a serious undertaking if you are just starting out, not least because you might have to stump up a hefty deposit or be tied into a lengthy or inflexible lease agreement.

Basically, I would not recommend leasing space as a start-up unless you are pretty sure of how much money you can make and can agree generous terms with the landlord. It can also help if you can split the risk with someone else, provided you are certain their income is guaranteed.

> **Taking out a lease can represent a major overhead and it is worth checking your figures, or getting them checked by an accountant, to make sure your business will be able to support it. You might also want to get some legal advice on the lease agreement before signing it.**

Things worth considering if you are going to lease an office include:

◆ What will happen if the number of people in your business goes up or down?

◆ Is the office suitable for the equipment you need, such as computers and printers?

◆ How secure is it?

◆ Is it fit for purpose? (In other words, does the building comply with fire regulations? Was it designed as an office, or has it been adapted? and so on.)

◆ How easy is it to get to?

◆ What is the state of the common parts of the building?

Sub-letting or sharing a lease

Sub-letting office space or sharing a lease with another company is probably a better idea than taking out your own lease, for a number of reasons.

◆ You will probably be able to agree better terms.

◆ You may be able to share furniture, equipment and services with the other business.

◆ You may be able to carry out work for the other business.

◆ If the other business's services are complementary to yours, you may be able to refer clients to it, and vice versa.

◆ You will be more likely to experience the buzz of a traditional office.

◆ The other business may be able to help yours with finance or services.

Against these attractions, it is likely that you will have to sacrifice some flexibility as the future of your business will, to some extent, be tied into that of the business you are sub-letting from or sharing with.

> **The success of a sub-letting or shared lease arrangement often depends on how well you get on with the business you are sharing with. Having too much or too little in common may be detrimental.**

Serviced offices

Another low-risk option is to take out what is referred to as a 'licence fee' covering serviced office space from a specialist company. The leader in this field is Regus (www.regus.com); others may be more competitive, but you may find that published rates are open to negotiation.

There is a number of reasons for considering serviced offices:

◆ The up-front cost for a serviced office is likely to be much less than it would be for finding your own space, as furniture, computer cabling and so on are all provided.

◆ The deposit is normally two months' rent, compared with up to six months' for a standard lease.

◆ Some companies even offer a service which will allow you to work out the break-even point of taking out a licence fee with them.

- With a serviced office you can move in, set up and expand with a minimum of hassle. Some companies even have smart phone systems that can make your business appear multi-national in hours.

- You can often rent 'space' on the serviced office company's computer server, which, along with cabling, can save you a lot on technology costs.

- If anything goes wrong with the building, from a blocked sink to a breakdown in the air conditioning, you do not have to worry about getting it fixed.

Basic serviced offices have everything you would expect to find if you were working in a big company, from receptionists to photocopiers.

Top operators also have large conference rooms, video-conferencing systems and the ability for you to use other buildings in their network for work while travelling country-wide or internationally.

The bottom line with all of them, however, is that they let you focus on running your business.

> **Like most things, though, you pay for what you get. So you might want to shop around to see if you find a deal that provides just the things you think you will need.**

4. Working From Client Premises

It is not unusual for clients to expect you to work from their premises, for example because you need to be in close contact with other members of a team or because the documents they need you to work on cannot be accessed outside their organisation.

Obviously this gets round having to find a place to work and, if you are working on the client's computer systems, saves wear and tear on your own equipment. Against this, your travel costs are likely to go up (and you may not be able to recharge them) and you will be wasting money if you are paying for office space of your own.

From the outset, then, it is probably a good idea to establish whether your clients expect you to do most of your work from your own premises, or on theirs.

IR35

An important factor to bear in mind when working from client premises is whether you will fall foul of an HMRC (Her Majesty's Revenue and Customs) regulation called IR35, to do with whether workers providing personal services should be classed as employees or not.

HMRC introduced this legislation in 2000 as a way of closing a tax avoidance loophole, used mainly by IT workers, whereby employees would leave their jobs to set up their own business, then carry on doing their old work under the guise of 'independent consultants'. The benefit to consultants is that, as I will show in the next chapter, it is possible to pay less tax as a sole trader or by owning a company than one would as an employee. In addition, the employer pays less as it does not have to cover costs such as National Insurance.

IR35 was an attempt to clamp down on this practice by extending the definition of 'employee' to cover many workers who are not on the payroll and who, under the regulations, would henceforth have to be paid under the Pay As You Earn (PAYE) scheme, like traditional employees.

The problem is that the extended definition of what constitutes an employee is extremely fuzzy.

The precedents set by the small (but increasing) number of cases that have been contested in court have much to do with where, when and how long you work for a particular client. Although investigations so far have mostly been restricted to workers in IT, IR35 extends to other providers of personal services, potentially including copywriters.

For the record, some of the criteria used by the HMRC to determine if you should be deemed an employee under IR35 include whether:

◆ you generally work for one client at a time, rather than having a number of contracts

- you work set hours, or a given number of hours a week or a month

- you have to do the work yourself rather than being able to hire someone else to do the work for you

- someone can tell you at any time what to do or when and how to do it

- you are paid by the hour, week or month

- you get overtime pay

- you work at the premises of the person you work for, or at a place or places he or she decides.

The nature of an independent copywriter's work means that the answer to many of these questions may be 'yes', which, according to HMRC, means you would theoretically be an employee and have to be paid under PAYE.

Will this make a difference? It all depends on how much money you earn. If your earnings from a single client are under the higher tax rate threshold, getting paid via PAYE is unlikely to be much of a worry. It might even be advantageous, as at least you will be assured of receiving your money promptly.

On the other hand, if your income from a client is enough to 'attract' (as accountants say) higher rate tax, then being on PAYE will give you little or no scope to avoid it, so you could end up paying the tax man more than you need to. In such a case you might well want to review your working practices to make sure you fall outside the IR35 rules. To do this, you may need to prove that:

- you have a number of customers at the same time

- you have the final say in how you do the work for the client

- you can make a loss on the contract

- you provide the main items of equipment (computers, fax machines and so on) you need to do the job for the client, not just the small items, like pens and stationery, that many employees provide for themselves

◆ you are free to hire other people on your own terms to do the work you have taken on and if you do, they will be paid out of your own pocket

◆ you have to correct unsatisfactory work in your own time and at your own expense.

> As you may have gathered, IR35 is a complex and evolving area. If you are uncertain about where you stand, or what you might need to do under given circumstances, I would suggest speaking to your accountant, if you have one, or talking to your client's personnel or payroll department. There is also more information on the HMRC website, www.hmrc.gov.uk/ir35

5

Book Keeping for Copywriters

If you are typical of most copywriters, then this is probably the chapter you are dreading to read. A writer trades in words, not numbers, and the majority of copywriters that I have come across tend to view figures with suspicion, as something difficult to understand and potentially dangerous. It is not uncommon for otherwise gifted copywriters to completely ignore things like financial records and taxes, possibly in the hope they will go away. Needless to say, the result of this course of action (or inaction) is usually disastrous.

It need not be that way. While I would hesitate to call book keeping 'fun', it is usually a pretty straightforward affair at the level of the average self-employed trader. For the difficult bits, like filling in your tax return, you can hire an accountant for a few hundred pounds a year. And running a cash book can be a useful way of keeping track of how much money you are making (which can be gratifying when things are going well).

1. Where Do You Start?

There are several things you need to do fairly soon after you set up your business; certainly within the first couple of months or so.

◆ Get in touch with your local tax office (you can find it in the *Yellow Pages* under 'HM Revenue and Customs') within three months of starting and tell them you are self-employed (there is a £100 penalty for not doing so). They will give you a Unique Tax Reference (UTR) number, which some clients may demand to see before taking you on.

◆ If you are setting up a limited company, you need to register it with Companies House (see www.companieshouse.co.uk for more details). They will tell about how to file financial records relating to the business.

◆ If you are thinking of using an accountant, now is a good time to find one so they can talk to you about how to run your accounts, and advise you on other areas of setting up your business such as choosing a simple accounting software package, if you need one.

◆ If you have decided to register for VAT (see Chapter 2), you should get in touch with HMRC. Again, you can find the details for your local office in your phone book, under 'VAT'.

◆ Get into the habit of asking for receipts whenever you spend money on anything vaguely connected with your business, from stationery to computers, and keep them somewhere safe.

2. How Do Accounts Work?

You will hopefully be relieved to know that I am not an accountancy expert. You do not need to be one either. If you have run a business before, or even been involved in one on the financial side, then you probably have a good idea of basic accounting already. In which case, you can skip this section (and possibly this chapter) as it applies to people who have no previous experience and/or knowledge of putting together accounts for their business.

At the risk of stating the very obvious, here is how your finances should work.

◆ You charge clients money for the work you do, usually by means of an invoice, and this provides income for your business. Copies of your invoices, plus a note of when they were paid, form the basis of your income records.

◆ You also spend money on behalf of your business, on travel, equipment, stationery and so on. Generally your accountant and/or the taxman will need to see a receipt as proof of expenditure.

◆ You need to keep a record of all your income and all your expenditure in a cash book which contains the date and amount of each transaction, along with how it was paid and what it was for.

◆ At the end of your business year (which runs for 12 months but need not be the same as the calendar year) the sum of all expenses which are allowable against tax (which is not necessarily all your expenses) is deducted from the sum of your income.

◆ What is left is your net profit. The taxman works out how much you owe in tax based on this amount.

◆ The way you are taxed depends on what type of business you run: sole trader, partnership or limited company.

◆ As a sole trader, if you want, you can get the taxman to work out how much you owe. To do so, you need to submit a tax return by 30 September following the year being assessed and tick the section saying you want the tax calculation done for you.

◆ Alternatively you can work out the amount you owe yourself (or, more likely, get your accountant to work it out). In this case, you can complete the return online or get your accountant to complete a tax return and submit it to HMRC by 31 January following the year being assessed.

◆ The taxman will then check the calculation and send you a bill.

◆ *But* you must pay what you think you owe (according to your own or your accountant's calculations) by 31 January following the end of your financial year, regardless of whether you have had a bill or not.

◆ If you do not pay, you could be liable for a fine plus an interest charge on the amount the taxman thinks you owe.

◆ HMRC will assume your tax bill is going to stay the same in the following year and ask you for two payments on account, each of half the total.

◆ The first payment on account is due on 31 January following the year of assessment – the same date as your tax bill is due.

◆ What this means is that your first tax bill will not just be for your first year's tax; it will be for one and a half times that amount.

◆ The second payment on account is due by 31 July. At the end of your next financial year, the amount you have paid on account is offset against what you owe in tax. So if your tax bill has gone down, you may get a repayment from HMRC. If there is a significant decrease in your taxable profits you can ask the taxman to postpone the second payment on account.

◆ If your business is a partnership, you (or your accountant) will also need to prepare a partnership tax return which shows how much taxable income was made by the partnership and how it was split between each partner. Each partner still needs to complete a tax return.

◆ In other respects, partnership finances are similar to those of a sole trader. Payments are calculated in the same way and due at the same times.

◆ If you run a limited company and it falls within the Companies Act limits of a small company (which it almost certainly will, or else you would not be reading this book for advice), your accounts need to be prepared in the statutory format probably by an accountant. A copy must be sent to Companies House within 14 days of them being approved by the board of the company and within ten months of the company's year-end. Failure to do this is an offence for which directors can be held liable, and prosecuted.

◆ A limited company is liable for tax separately to its owners and employees. Corporation tax is a complex affair and it is always worth getting expert advice in relation to it.

◆ Value Added Tax is levied by HMRC and is completely separate from income and corporation tax. There are more details on how to deal with it later in this chapter.

◆ National Insurance Contributions (NICs) are yet another levy which you have to be aware of. If you are self-employed, either as a sole trader or within a partnership, then you have to pay Class 2 NICs, which are a fixed amount payable quarterly or monthly by direct debit, plus Class 4 NICs, which are calculated as a percentage of your profits between set limits.

3. Your Financial Year

It goes without saying that your financial year lasts 12 months. But when it starts and ends is up to you. You can simply take the beginning of your financial year to be the date you start your business. Or, if it is more convenient, you can choose to complete accounts for part of a year in your first year, up to whenever you want your financial year to start, and then file a return every 12 months thereafter.

Probably the best reason for changing your financial year is so that it fits in with the UK tax year, which runs from 6 April to 5 April. (Corporation tax, however, is based on a financial year that runs from 1 April to 31 March.) The beginning of the tax year is when the chancellor usually chooses to make changes to tax legislation, so adopting the same calendar will at least prevent you from having to take account of different laws in a single year.

4. Receipts

Keep all receipts to do with your business. Get into the habit of asking for receipts whenever you buy things, from computers to biros. When you travel, keep your bus or train ticket in lieu of a receipt. If you work from home, hang on to household bills for gas, electricity and so on. Keep your phone bill, your mobile bill and credit card statements listing

Cash book: receipts for June

Date	Customer	Notes	Other	Sales	Cash	Bank
12/6	Bloggs Industries	Payment of inv. No. 237	105.10	1,225.00		1,330.10
27/6	Bloggs.com	Payment of inv. No. 231	3.38	500.00		503.38
Totals			**108.48**	**1,725.00**	**0.00**	**1,833.48**

Fig. 1. Cash book entry example: receipts page.

business-related expenses like internet service provider subscriptions. Keep all receipts. Got that?

The reason is that these will all add up to reduce your net profit, and hence your tax bill. Or, look at it another way: every expense that you incur and which you cannot show a receipt for will be considered profit. And you will still be taxed on it.

File your receipts in date order and enter the details into your cash book. You can buy ruled books for this purpose if you want to keep handwritten records, but in this day and age you are more likely to use a computer spreadsheet such as Microsoft Excel. An example of how pages in your cash book might look are shown in Figures 1 and 2.

Unfortunately, you cannot claim all your business expenses against tax. And not all expenses are offset in the same way. Items which will last for a long period of time, such as computers, computer software and office furniture, are treated as *capital expenses*. Unlike the running costs of your business, for things like travel or stationery, these are spread out over several years. So, for example, you will not be able to offset the entire price of your shiny new computer against tax in the year you buy it (although, if you are registered for VAT you will be able to reclaim this entire element of the cost). At the time of writing, there is a tax concession called First Year Capital Allowances for small businesses which allows you to set off 50 per cent of the cost of IT equipment against your profits in the year of purchase. However, HMRC might withdraw or reduce this concession in the future.

The main items you can claim against tax are as follows.

◆ **Staff costs**, whether you employ people on a full-time basis or hire people to help you out once in a while. You can also pay your partner if they help out with your business, for example with book keeping. If your partner does not have other employment, this can be a handy way of cutting your tax bill as you can use up their basic tax allowance (the amount of money each person is entitled to earn free of tax).

◆ **Premises costs**, such as electricity, gas, rent or mortgage interest and telephone rental. If you work from home, the taxman will expect you to claim a proportion of your annual premises costs that reflects the amount your home is used for business. So, for example, if you have five rooms in your home (including any room where you could fit a desk, such as kitchens, living rooms and bedrooms, but excluding bathrooms), and work entirely from home, you would be justified in claiming up to a fifth of your household bills against tax. Commonly, a set weekly amount is used for calculating a 'use of home as office' charge.

◆ You can also claim back **repairs to your office space**, even if it is just a room in your house. Be aware, though, this does not mean you can offset the cost of redecorating your entire home. As with other household expenses, the taxman will allow only a proportion of costs that can be attributed directly to your workplace. Note, also, that repairs are not the same as improvements. The latter, according to the HMRC, will increase the value of your workspace and, if you own it, will mean you could be liable for capital gains tax on a proportion of the profits if and when you sell it.

◆ **General administrative expenses** incurred in the day-to-day running of your business. These will include phone bills; postage, photocopying and stationery; couriers, if you use them; the cost of magazines, newspapers and other reference materials; subscriptions to publications and services

Cash book: payments for June

Date	Supplier	Cheque	Bank	Cash	Staff	Premises	Repairs	General administrative expenses						
					Wages	Light/Heat	Repairs	Phone	Post/print stationery	Couriers	Journals & reference	Subscrip-tions	Insurances	General office	Other admin costs
05/6	GNER	Switch card	9.5												
07/6	Easyjet	Switch card	63.4												
09/6	Easyjet	Switch card	82.5												
12/6	EDF Energy	Cheque number 100044	11.0			11.02									
17/6	Npower	Cheque number 100046	3.1			3.16									
18/6	O2	Cheque number 100047	162.0					158.55					3.49		
19/6	Bank	Bank debit	0.1												
21/6	British Rail			2.20											
21/6	British Rail			8.90											
21/6	taxi			10.00											
21/6	taxi			20.00											
21/6	taxi			13.00											
21/6	London Underground			1.60											
24/6	TalkTalk	Direct debit	36.4					36.43							
24/6	Thameslink Rail	Switch	9.8												
27/6	taxi			6.20											
27/6	British Rail			10.00											
Sub-totals			378.0	71.90	0.00	14.18	0.00	194.98	0.00	0.00	0.00	0.00	3.49	0.00	0.00
Totals				449.98											

Fig. 2. Cash book entry example: payments page.

Motor expenses					Travel & subsistence			Promotion		Professional costs		Finance costs		Sundry	
Petrol	Servicing	Insurance	Road tax/ parking/AA	Hire & leasing charges	Rail/taxi/air & bus fares	Hotel/acco-modation	Subsistence	Advertising & promotion	Entertaining	Accountancy fees	Other fees	Bank charges	Credit card charges	Other expenses	Notes
					9.50										Train fare
					63.46										Air fare
					82.50										Air fare
															final electricity bill
															Final gas bill
															Mobile phone bill
												0.17			Bank account interest
					2.20										Train fare
					8.90										Train fare
					10.00										taxi fare
					20.00										taxi fare
					13.00										taxi fare
					1.60										Tube fare
															Business phone calls
					9.80										Train fare
					6.20										taxi fare
					10.00										Train fare
0.00	0.00	0.00	0.00	0.00	237.16	0.00	0.00	0.00	0.00	0.00	0.00	0.17	0.00	0.00	
														449.98	

Fig. 2. (cont.)

like internet access; insurance costs; equipment repairs and leasing; and anything else you buy for your office.

◆ **Car expenses**, such as petrol, motor insurance, membership of motoring organisations, or hire charges, can also be allowed, although the taxman will presume that there will be some personal mileage. If you use your car for work a lot, keep a record of business mileage and work out, realistically, what proportion of the total mileage this represents. Use this percentage to calculate the business element of your car expenses. If you are VAT registered and you reclaim all the input VAT on all your petrol expenses you will be liable to pay a set quarterly petrol scale charge to HMRC, to cover any private mileage. Alternatively, you could use HMRC's set business mileage rates of 40p per mile for the first 10,000 miles and 25p per mile thereafter.

◆ **All travel costs**, including bus, train, taxi and plane fares and overnight stays in hotels or guesthouses, as long as they are directly related to business. Similarly, if you travel around the country or abroad and the trip involves an element of work, you can claim expenses that reflect that element. You can also claim meals as long as they are necessarily a part of work-related travel. One criterion I have heard of to judge this is that they have to be incurred outside of a five mile radius from your normal place of work.

◆ **Promotional costs** incurred in advertising your business. This can include the cost of setting up a website, for example. Unfortunately, however, one of the major expenses you are likely to come across in promoting your business – the cost of networking, lunching with or entertaining clients and contacts – cannot be claimed against tax. Also, no input VAT can be reclaimed on entertaining.

◆ **Professional costs**, including accountants' fees (your accountant will probably be quick to point out that their payment is tax-deductible) and those of lawyers, if you use them.

◆ **Finance expenses**, such as charges and interest on business bank accounts, credit cards, hire purchase or loans, but not capital repayments.

◆ **Your pension payments**. You would not normally include these in your cash book, but they should be entered on your tax return. Whatever you do, it is important you set some money aside for your pension if you intend to stay in business for any length of time, as no one else will. A stakeholder pension is likely to be the best option because it is cheap to run and simple to set up. For more advice, speak to your independent financial adviser, if you have one. You can also get information from financial websites like The Motley Fool (www.fool.co.uk).

> **Things you cannot claim against tax, no matter how vital they may be to the livelihood of your business, include entertainment, food and drink (except for subsistence incurred in business-related travel) and gifts, unless they carry your company logo.**

5. Invoices

Your invoices should show the following details:

◆ Your trading name and, if you run a registered company, your company number.

◆ Your address and other contact details, such as phone number, fax and email address.

◆ The date the invoice was issued.

◆ An invoice number. You can use any numbering system you want but it is a good idea to have one that allows you to identify the client, month and year each invoice relates to. HMRC usually requires some sort of sequentially numbered system so it is easy to see if invoices have been omitted.

◆ The date the work refers to. This will usually be the date a project is finished and delivered to the client, unless you have an agreement to be paid in advance.

Invoice

Bloggs Copywriting Service
100 Any Road
Anytown

30 May 200X

Invoice no. 010

To: Any Communications
                200 Another Road
                Anytown

For: Freelance services in May

5 days @ £200 per day: £1,000.00

Plus expenses – train fare   £10.00

Fig. 3. Invoice example.

◆ Details of the work carried out. If you are being paid by the day or by the word, then put the total number of days or words and the rate of pay.

◆ Details of any costs or disbursements you are recharging to the client. Some clients may be happy for you to bill them for any costs incurred on their behalf, such as phone calls or travel. Others may expect you to shoulder these costs within your fee. (For simplicity's sake, I normally include phone calls and other basic costs in my fee, but recharge larger expenses such as taxi or train fares.)

◆ The total amount due.

◆ Your terms. Most clients will expect 30 days and are unlikely to pay any earlier, but sticking to these terms at least gives you a good excuse to chase accounts departments that you fear may be delaying payment.

◆ If you are VAT registered, you need to include your VAT number on each invoice. You also need to show a subtotal of all fees and costs, then the VAT due on the subtotal, which, for copywriting services, will be at the standard rate of 17.5 per cent at the time of writing.

You may also want to include mention of any prompt payment discounts (see 'Managing cash flow' below) and your bank account details, for clients that pay electronically through the Banks Automated Clearing System (BACS). An example of an invoice is shown in Figure 3. You will be able to get others in leaflets from your local HMRC office.

6. Managing Cash Flow

Managing cash flow is simple: get money in as soon as you can and hang on to it for as long as possible. Although this might not seem too important when you have plenty of projects on the go and are working flat out to meet deadlines, it is a crucial task in running a business. Your clients will certainly take it seriously (as well they might, since cash flow problems can cripple the healthiest of companies), with the knock-on effect that you might have to wait a lot longer to get paid than you expect. There is a number of things you can do to keep on top of your cash flow.

◆ Invoice early. If not as soon as you finish a job, then at least by the end of the month.

◆ If you are working on a project that will take some time to complete, ask to be paid in instalments – every month, for example.

◆ If you have any reason to suspect your client might take a long time to pay (or not pay at all), you may want to insist on payment or part-payment up front.

◆ Give clients an incentive to pay up quickly, such as a five per cent discount on invoices settled within seven days. Smaller, owner-managed companies often appreciate this kind of deal.

◆ Keep an eye out for invoices that have not been paid after 30 days and do not be afraid to chase up settlement. Often a polite call or email asking whether the invoice has been cleared for payment will be enough to prompt a cheque.

◆ Be prepared to step up the pressure if you have still not been paid after a couple of months. Many copywriters worry that hounding their clients will spoil the relationship they have built up and jeopardise their chances of future work. But you have to ask yourself what value there is in a client who will not pay you.

◆ As a last resort, consider demanding interest on any late payment (which you are legally entitled to do) or threatening to take the matter to the small claims court. I have yet to hear of a copywriter actually making good on such a threat, but if you ever have to, then bear in mind that it will probably help your case if you have kept copies of all relevant correspondence.

◆ Pay cheques into your account the day you get them.

◆ Take time to find out how you can smooth out the payment process with your client. Many companies, for example, have problems processing invoices unless they quote the number of a purchase order raised by the person making the order.

◆ Some clients may want you to add your bank details to their supplier list so they can pay you electronically. This is good. If you are on the system you are much more likely to get paid on time.

◆ I personally do not advocate delaying payment to your own suppliers unless you really have to; after all, you may well have to ask them for favours in the future. But do take advantage of any opportunity to hang on to your cash, for example by paying for a new computer in instalments.

If all the above seems like too much hassle, consider the following story regarding a copywriter friend of mine, Gareth Llewellyn. In the late 1990s Gareth started writing occasional features for a website whose managers he got on with particularly well. The work increased and Gareth concentrated on meeting deadlines rather than sending out invoices. Then the website started to run into trouble and Gareth suddenly realised he was owed quite a lot of money – around £5,000, which he was by then relying on to pay his tax bill – and had yet to see any of it. In the end, it was over a year before the bill was settled. 'The bank and the taxman were unhappy with me to say the least,' he says. 'The principle is, don't do the next piece of work until the first is paid for.'

> There is some good news, however. Copywriting businesses are relatively immune to cash flow problems because their costs are fairly low (or, to put it another way, the margins are very high).

7. Choosing an Accountant

You do not need an accountant for your business, but you may well find it helps, particularly if you anticipate making a fair amount of money. A good accountant should be able to repay their fee by making suggestions that can help cut your tax bill, and will be able to advise you on other areas of your business, too. He or she can also make sure your tax returns are correct and let you know which allowances you can claim for.

The level of service you will get from your accountant will usually depend on how much you pay them. You should be able to find someone who will check your books and fill out your tax return for around £500 a year, plus

VAT. For an extra (generally small) fee, an accountancy practice may be able to put together your books from your receipts and other basic information, although you may feel it is a better idea to run your own cash book as a way of keeping an eye on your finances.

One thing that is worth bearing in mind if you decide to take on an accountant is whether they have any relevant experience in your industry. Effectively, your accountant will be responsible for negotiating on behalf of your business with the tax man, so it helps if they know in advance what kinds of allowances HMRC will make.

Ask other copywriters, if you know any, who they would recommend. Alternatively, look for ads in magazines like *The Freelance*, published by the London Freelance Branch of the National Union of Journalists, or UK *Press Gazette*.

If you cannot find someone who already handles people in your line of business, do not despair. Any good accountant should still be able to help you save tax. However, it is still worth shopping around to make sure you find an adviser you feel you can get on with. If all else fails, your local *Yellow Pages* should give you some names to get started with.

8. Filing Your Own Tax Returns

There is nothing to stop you filling out your own tax returns. If your income is fairly low, say because you work only part-time, and your accounts are straightforward, it is probably safe to assume you will not save much by hiring an accountant.

The easiest option under these circumstances is to get the tax man to work out how much you owe, by filling out the forms provided by HMRC. You need to return these before 30 September each year.

If you decide to be your own accountant, you will generally find HMRC is happy to help and advise you on what you can and cannot allow against tax. You may also find that much of what is allowed is based on negotiation with the authorities, rather than any hard and fast rules.

It is also fairly simple to register with the Government Gateway (www.gateway.gov.uk) with a user name and password. You will get a PIN and then be able to complete your tax return online at www.hmrc.gov.uk. When you have entered all your details the program calculates the tax you owe. You can save the information and go back to it as often as you like if you need to change figures or add further details. Print it out and make sure you submit it by 31 January.

9. National Insurance

How you pay National Insurance Contributions (NICs) will depend on how you have set up your business.

If you run a limited company, you will pay yourself a monthly wage under Pay As You Earn and NICs will be added to this as with any other employee.

If you are self employed as a sole trader or a partner in a business, you usually pay two different types of NIC, called Class 2 and Class 4. Class 2 NICs are set at a flat rate per month which you can pay by monthly direct debit or quarterly bill. Bills are sent to you automatically after you register as self-employed with the tax office. Class 4 NICs are paid on top of Class 2 NICs if your profits are over a certain amount (around £5,255 a year) up to around £34,840 (these bands are usually increased every year so check with HMRC). The amount you pay is worked out as a percentage (eight per cent at the time of writing) of your profits between the upper and lower limits.

If you want or need to find out more about NICs, including exemptions, there is a useful guide called *National Insurance Contributions for Self-employed People with Small Earnings* that you can download from www.hmrc.gov.uk or get hold of from your tax office by quoting leaflet reference CF10.

10. VAT

Value Added Tax (VAT) is a completely separate tax from income tax. You have to register for VAT if your turnover is more than £64,000 a year, but can choose to register voluntarily at less than this amount.

VAT account

Period from 1 January to 31 March, 2008

VAT deductible – input tax	£	VAT payable – output tax	£
January	54.38	January	545.19
February	62.66	February	1,025.23
March	26.59	March	781.32
Total	143.63	Total	2,351.74
VAT allowable on EC acquisitions	–	VAT due on EC acquisitions	–
Net over-claim of input tax from previous returns	–	Net understatement of output tax on previous returns	–
Bad debt relief	–	Annual adjustment: Direct Calculation scheme	–
Sub-total	143.63	Sub-total	2,351.74
Less:		Less:	
VAT on credits received from suppliers	–	VAT on credits allowed to customers	–
Total tax deductible	143.63	Total tax to pay	2,351.74
		Less total tax deductible	143.63
		Payable to Revenue and Customs	2,208.11

Fig. 4. VAT account example.

Once registered, you can claim back the VAT you pay on supplies, provided you have a VAT receipt for them. You also have to add VAT to any supplies you make in the UK, which includes all fees and expenses you incur on behalf of a client. The VAT on copywriting is levied at the standard rate, 17.5 per cent at the time of writing. Your invoices will need to show your VAT number, and every three months you will have to prepare a VAT account, which is a short summary showing how much money you are claiming back and how much you have added on. (Since 2002 there has also been an optional flat-rate VAT scheme allowing companies with a turnover of up to £150,000 to calculate their VAT payment as a given percentage, 9.5 per cent for advertising, of their total taxable turnover including VAT at 17.5 per cent. To find out more, ask your VAT office for a copy of Notice 733 or download it from www.hmrc.gov.uk). You then need to complete a VAT return and send it, along with the balance of your account, if you owe money, to HMRC. An example of a quarterly VAT account is shown in Figure 4.

If that all sounds a bit complicated, do not worry. Compared with income tax, VAT is easy, and is something you would probably deal with yourself rather than handing to your accountant. However, having to deal with it every three months can still be a chore, so it is debatable how much benefit you would get from registering if you do not really have to.

Do not worry about clients being put off by adding VAT to your invoices. They will just reclaim the 17.5 per cent charged from HMRC, as you do with your own receipts.

6

How to Find Work – and Keep It

1. Sources of Income

Where will your work come from? This question is not just one you will ask
yourself as you start out in business, but one that will present itself for as
long as you trade. It is quite likely that you will already have part of the
answer; a big contract that is yours for the taking, for example, or access to a
network of contacts that will assure you of a steady stream of jobs.

Most likely this promise of work is from an existing contact, someone you
already have a long-standing relationship with. This is where most of all
freelance copywriters' work comes from. Even if you do not have any work
leads yet, you should be aware that they will mostly come from people you
know. These are the people who are always more likely to trust your abilities
and bear you in mind.

How else do you drum up business? Some options to consider are:

◆ advertising your services

◆ using the web to find work

◆ working through agencies.

> This chapter will guide you through the intricacies of each, plus
> everything you need to know about pitching for business, from
> presentations to pricing.

2. Networking

If your most likely source of income is going to be people you know (and, believe me, it usually is) then go out and talk to them. Do not be afraid to mention, brazenly, to anyone you know who might be interested, that you will be happy to take care of their copywriting needs. Some of them might even take up your offer. And if not, at least they will be more likely to recommend you if they hear of a copywriting job elsewhere.

Running a copywriting business means you need to become an expert in networking, the art of making and keeping contacts. There is a general, although not universal, rule that the longer you work the easier it is to get new work. This is because, over time, and assuming your work is of decent enough quality, more and more people will come to know about you, either directly or through referrals, and call upon you for help. In order to get the ball rolling, you have to work hard at building up a network of contacts.

This is why it is often easier to start up in business after working in a company within the creative or media industries, where you are likely to come across a number of individuals or organisations that could use your services.

3. Advertising and Promotion

As a copywriter, I would be among the first to underline the power of advertising and promotion. However, I have to say I do not know of anyone who has been able to rely on these methods alone to drum up an income from writing. Although I am willing to be proved wrong, my view is that advertising and promotion can be used only to supplement networking as a way of bringing in new work.

In addition, the success of any promotional campaign is largely based on two factors: whether the medium you use reaches people who will be interested in your service; and then whether the promotional message appeals to these people and induces them to contact you for more information. Finding what works is often a process of trial and error, so, in theory, you can end up spending a lot of money without generating any business.

For that reason, if you are going to try advertising I would recommend looking at low-cost options that are guaranteed to reach a useful audience. Here are some suggestions:

♦ Try advertising in local business publications (rather than the local paper or *Yellow Pages*) such as the Chamber of Commerce magazine.

♦ Get listed on as many freelance directories as possible. A good one to start with is at www.mad.co.uk, the marketing, advertising and design website run by Centaur, publisher of *Marketing Week*, *Precision Marketing* and other relevant trade magazines. (For more on promoting yourself on the web, see below.)

♦ Consider a direct mail campaign, writing to local businesses to offer your services. Needless to say, your letter will need to have all the ingredients of a great mail-shot: good writing, creativity and an alluring offer. There are pointers to all this in Part 2 of this book.

> **Keep track of what you spend on promotion to make sure that you are getting value for money out of it.**

4. Finding Work on the Web

The internet is incredibly useful (some might say indispensable) as a research tool for copywriting and it also generates a lot of copy work, both for websites and other types of online media. This does not mean, unfortunately, that the web can bring you work in abundance. You still have to go out and get it using traditional methods. In my experience you can put a lot of time, effort and money into promoting yourself on the internet and get very little in return.

Broadly speaking, there are three ways in which you can use the web to find work:

◆ by simply using it as a research tool to identify potential clients

◆ by signing up to online freelance work exchanges

◆ by building your own website and trying to direct potential clients to it via search engines, online advertising and other methods.

Using the web as a research tool

If there is one thing the internet is good for, then it has to be research. And that applies as much to the work you are doing as to new sources of work. At the very least, the web can give you access to up-to-date company information such as addresses, phone numbers, emails, personnel and organisational structures. Use it to find out more about companies you think you could work for. Check their press pages to see if they employ a PR agency that might be interested in your writing skills. Do they have a customer magazine you could contribute to? Is it worth talking to the marketing director about the content of the website itself? Does their job application page mention whether they need freelance writing help?

Like any form of research, however, trawling the internet can be very time-consuming unless you have a good idea of what you are looking for. I would advise using web research as part of a wider, structured plan for finding new business. You might decide, for example, to approach all the direct mail companies listed in your local *Yellow Pages*, in which case checking their websites would be a good way to get extra information about their businesses.

Signing up to online work exchanges

A number of websites, such as E-lance, Guru and Smarterwork, act as freelance work exchanges where clients can post projects for which contractors then bid.

These exchanges are generally subscription-based and levy a percentage of each transaction that is carried out on them (almost all have some inbuilt secure payment system through which projects are paid for).

In theory, they sound like a great idea: just sign up and bid for as many projects as you like, from the comfort of your office. Like many other great dotcom concepts, however, these services are not quite so great in practice. The problem is that while the concept is an obvious winner for freelancers of all shapes, sizes and abilities, clients are perhaps more wary of putting valuable projects out to tender to people about whom they have little or no knowledge.

The upshot is that both the value and the number of copywriting projects that get posted on these exchanges tend to be quite low and the number of bidders is very high, often running to dozens. Faced with a barrage of offers for help, often with widely ranging price tags, it seems likely that most clients simply opt for those specialists who have been registered with the website longest and thus can prove their ability on the basis of ratings provided by other project owners. As a result, your chances of winning a bid tend to be about ten to one at best; much less than you would find as a copywriter in virtually any other competitive tendering situation. Furthermore, to increase your chances of winning the work you may well be tempted to try to undercut other bidders, so that even if you win the project it is likely to be far from profitable.

As part of the research for this book I subscribed to one of these websites, Smarterwork (www.smarterwork.com), and 'pitched' for at least one project a month over the course of more than six months. Many of these projects were exactly the kind of assignments that my regular clients were (and still are) handing to me, without a pitch, on a routine basis. Despite spending a lot of time pitching for projects on Smarterwork, however, I never made a penny from the service.

In summary, while there is obviously no harm in signing up to online work exchanges (provided they do not charge you too much upfront), I would be very wary of assuming that you can make a living from them. Not only that, but the paucity of projects on many of these exchanges makes me wonder how many of them will still be around by the time you read this chapter.

Using a website to promote yourself

Having your own website is far from a necessity in marketing your services, but can be a handy way of giving people access to your credentials, and is particularly likely to impress clients if you expect to do a lot of work for companies in the technology sector.

Building a website is a big enough subject to warrant its own book; and, happily, there are plenty of good reference books out there. Essentially, you will need to go through the following steps:

◆ Find somewhere that will house (or 'host') your site. If you use an internet services provider (ISP) to surf the net then you will probably find they provide a certain amount of space for personal websites. However, there may be restrictions on the website addresses you can use. For a more professional approach, you will probably want to have a domain name of your own choosing, which you can buy (provided it has not already been taken by someone else) from a domain name registration service such as Netnames (www.netnames.com). These will often be able to host your site, too, for a fee.

◆ Get your site built. If you fancy the challenge, you can teach yourself HTML (hypertext mark-up language, the code commonly used to put together simple websites) and build your own. HTML is not too complicated and you could pick up enough of a grasp of it to get going in just a few weeks; a good book for beginners is *Teach Yourself HTML* (IDC Books). Nowadays, however, there is a number of web authoring software packages, such as Dreamweaver from Macromedia or Microsoft FrontPage, that make the process even easier. Be aware, however, the results can be somewhat formulaic. The other option is to get a friendly website designer to help you out, or pay for them to do the job. They may even be able to take care of domain name registration and hosting for you.

◆ Promote your site on search engines and via links to other sites. Web marketing is another big area about which much has been written.

Points worth bearing in mind with regard to websites are:

◆ Having a website does not guarantee an immediate listing on search engines. You can submit your site for a listing on each search engine (details of how to do this are usually to be found on a link from the search engine home page), although some may try to get you to pay for this – but even then, there are no guarantees your site will be listed.

◆ If you are going to shell out for a search engine listing, you might be better off putting the money into a service such as Google AdWords, which effectively buys you a listing whenever a specified search phrase is keyed in. And you pay only when someone clicks through the link.

◆ A further, free way of improving your chances of being found on the web is to get as many other sites as possible to link to yours. 'Spiders', the programs used by search engines to map the internet, use links as routes to find new sites, so your chances of getting a listing will be increased if other websites are linked to yours. To do this, though, you will either need to be friendly with a lot of webmasters or, better still, offer something of value that others feel is worth linking to.

◆ It goes without saying that no matter how simple or complex the design of your site, the way it is written is crucial. For inspiration, I suggest you key 'copywriting services' into a search engine and take a look at what your competitors are saying. A couple of US copywriters whose sites have impressed me are Ivan Levison (www.levison.com) and Nick Usborne (www.nickusborne.com); there are many more out there worth a look.

Make sure you read Chapter 13 – Writing for the Internet – before drafting the copy for your website.

5. Working Through Agencies

Some recruitment agencies in the media and communications sectors have units that specialise in placing freelancers. If you are starting out and/or do not have a ready source of work, these can be a good bet, but bear in mind the rates you can expect may be lower than those you could get from selling your services directly, since the agency will take a cut of your fees. To track down agencies that might be able to find work for you, take a look at the display advertising sections of industry magazines such as *Marketing*, *Marketing Week* and *Campaign*. Two agencies which operate sizeable freelance departments are Stop Gap and Major Players. Bear in mind that you will need to be able to give them a CV. Also, it may be difficult to find recruitment companies that specialise in this kind of business outside London.

Is freelance work advertised in the press?

Yes, but infrequently. And it is usually placed by agencies such as those described above. In general, the cost of display advertising means companies will not use it to recruit freelancers unless they are looking to fill a long-term contract. Companies like the BBC often advertise contracts and may occasionally offer jobs for copywriters. Other opportunities can arise from time to time; the best places to look are in the weekly media section of *The Guardian* newspaper and its associated website, http://media.guardian.co.uk, plus the main marketing, media and creative magazines and websites: *Marketing*, *Marketing Week*, *Campaign*, www.campaignlive.com, www.brandrepublic.com, www.mad.co.uk and others. You will probably have to subscribe to most of these, although the cost is at least tax-deductible.

6. Drumming up Business over the Phone

In his book *The Well-Fed Writer*, US copywriter Peter Bowerman advocates kick-starting your copywriting business with a sustained telemarketing campaign. The idea is that if you introduce yourself to as many potential clients as possible, some are eventually likely to give you work. Bowerman's technique involves setting yourself a target number of calls (say up to 50 a day, perhaps culled from the business phone book), write a short introductory script and keep plugging away to build up a list of contacts, following up with mail shots and personal visits once a lead gets warm. I cannot vouch for the approach personally since I have not used it. But what I can say is that if you are hoping to get started in copywriting the work will not come to you of its own accord. You have to go out there and get it. So if you are at loose end, putting in calls to people who might be interested in your services can only be a good thing.

7. Pitching, Impressing, Winning and Pricing

Whichever way you end up finding work, it is unlikely to be handed to you on a plate. You will normally have to convince a prospective client that you are up to the job and that your fee will fit their budget.

Putting together a portfolio

Generally speaking, the measure of how good you are is in the work you have already done. Consequently, it is worth building up a portfolio and/or a résumé of your work that you can send to prospective clients. (This is also the sort of information you will want to include on your website, if you have one.)

Try to make sure you get a copy of all the work you do, even down to the smallest flyer. Few clients will want to see all of it, but you could frequently be called upon to show your expertise in particular areas – writing newsletters, for example – so it is useful to have more than one example to hand. Your 'portfolio', therefore, should not be a collection of randomly-assembled work, but a selection of the copy you have written that you think is most suited to a particular job.

If you have a CV or résumé, it is similarly a good idea to tailor it to different types of work. Also, remember that you are not looking for a permanent job, so you should not structure the document in the same way as you would write a traditional CV. Make sure it brings out your relevant experience first and forget about making a big deal about which university you went to or what your hobbies are. The important points are which other clients you have worked for and what you have done for them.

In the early days it will obviously be difficult to come up with a dazzling client list and a long list of projects, so feel free to include examples of writing work you may have done in previous jobs or during any relevant training courses.

If you are really stuck, it might be worth considering some free work for friends and acquaintances, as a way of building up a portfolio. It might also help you build up a network of contacts who can offer paying jobs.

Pitching for work

If you have worked in any form of marketing communications agency, then you will probably be familiar with the process of pitching: brainstorming ideas, putting together creative executions and a pitch document, rehearsing the presentation and assembling a team to represent the business.

Thankfully, copywriters are rarely required to go to such lengths. Copywriting work is (sadly) not normally high value enough to warrant a major pitch and because freelance copywriters are fairly rare you are unlikely to be facing much competition. At most, you are likely to be asked to meet the client for a briefing, put forward some thoughts on your approach and provide a quote for the work. Even so, you have to make sure you land the job. So what do you do?

◆ When you meet the client, show that you understand their business. Dress appropriately: jeans might be OK for a dotcom but make sure you are in a suit and tie if you are visiting a stock broker. Tell them about any clients you have worked for in the same or related industries. Research their industry, if you need to, so you are aware of the issues affecting them. Make sure you can understand their jargon. (But if you do not, then by all means ask for clarification. After all, you need to know what you are talking about if you are going to make an educated guess at the kind of work involved and how much it will cost.)

◆ When you put forward a proposal, make sure it meets the client's requirements. Your idea may be creative, but will it have the desired effect? Have you taken account of any sensitivities or issues regarding the project? Is your proposed approach in keeping with tone of the organisation issuing it?

◆ When you quote for the work, is it an amount that the client will be happy with? And will it be enough to justify your time and effort? (See below for more on pricing.)

Taking a brief

Knowing how to take a brief is important if you want to win business and write copy that meets your client's expectations. Make sure you:

◆ Ask lots of questions. Your client should do most of the talking, not you.

◆ Narrow down, as far as possible, exactly what is involved: how many pages, how many words, how many versions and so on.

◆ Clarify how many re-writes might be expected.

◆ Establish whether there are any concerns or sensitivities that you need to be aware of. Pharmaceutical companies, for example, are very restricted in what they can claim in advertising.

◆ Find out when the work needs to be delivered.

◆ Get an idea of the budget, if there is one.

◆ Try out any 'on the spot' ideas you might have, to see whether the client is likely to be in tune with particular lines of thinking.

Pricing

What level should you price yourself at? Answering this question is not always easy. Go too high and clients might decide they cannot afford you. Go too low and you could find you cannot pay the rent.

To work out what you could charge, you could try doing some research. A good place to start might be by talking to specialist agencies, signing up to an online work exchange (see above) or looking at the fees posted on the National Union of Journalists' website (www.londonfreelance.org/feesguide/) to see what other people are asking for. This may not help you much, however. There can be a tremendous range of prices quoted for similar jobs, usually starting at £100 to £150 a day and going up to two or three times that amount.

The reason fee levels vary so much is simple: it is entirely up to you to set your price and you can go as high or as low as you want. You could, theoretically, produce a figure off the top of your head. But there is a better way.

The trick is not to ask yourself what price your work should be, but how much it is worth – to you and *to your client.* This process can help you work out a happy medium that will be right for both parties. Remember that, as your own boss, you do not have to stick to a rigid price level and can chop and change your rates, within reason, to suit particular circumstances.

To work out what a job is worth to you, first calculate what your minimum fee level should be, with reference to the section on business plans in Chapter 2. Ideally, you will want to earn a bit more than this, but you may decide that some types of work are worth taking on at break-even point, or even at a discount. If you are keen on journalism, for example, you might feel happy about taking on news or feature writing commissions even though they are paid at lower rates than other jobs. By the same token, be realistic about what you quote for projects that look as if they will be difficult or complicated.

Get into the knack, also, of working out roughly what the value of your work is to your client. A rush job that needs to be done urgently over the weekend is going to be worth more than a non-vital project that the client could just as easily do in-house.

Price is an important part of winning business, but it is always much better to negotiate on the basis of value. If you keep worrying whether the level of your fees is too high, you will probably end up under-pricing yourself. Instead, ask yourself what justifies the fee that you think is fair. Can you turn the work around extra fast? Have you got experience that your client would value and that they would not easily find elsewhere? Will you manage the project as well as writing copy? Your client will probably value things like this and be prepared to pay a premium for them.

Conversely, if the client's budget allows for less than you would expect to be paid, it is usually better to see if you can cut the workload accordingly rather than simply dropping your price. You might get the client to take care of any necessary approvals, for example, or undertake just to carry out the essential parts of the project until or unless extra cash is available.

Another thing you might want to try is to use price negotiations to improve your cash flow. If your client insists on a cheaper deal, for example, offer a prompt payment discount if your bills are paid within seven days. That way you both benefit.

There is a good reason why your client should appreciate you being honest and forthright about pricing. If you are happy with what you are being paid for a job, it will act as a good incentive for you to spend time on it and do it well. Taking on low-paid work, however, could force you to cut corners, which will benefit neither you nor your client in the long run. This is why it is always better to work on the basis of value, rather than price.

> **Remember that the object of the negotiation process is not to get the work at any price, but to get the work at a price which both you and the client are happy with.**

How do you charge?

There are two main ways of charging fees: by time (usually on an hourly or day-rate basis) or by word count. The former is common in agency circles, the latter is more characteristic of press journalism, but in effect the two are interchangeable and you can use them both, even for different jobs with the same client.

The important point is that the system you use works for you and your client. A word count fee might be appropriate, for example, where you have to deliver a document of a given length but are not sure how long it will take. Working on a day-rate basis might be better if you are doing regular work for a client, such as writing ads or press releases.

If in doubt, you might want to offer the client the choice of which type of rate they prefer. You will however need to be sure that you are costing the work on a roughly like-for-like basis using each method.

Two variations on these approaches are to quote a flat fee for a project, or to ask for a retainer, both worked out on a rough calculation of the amount of time the job is likely to take.

These methods are generally more appropriate to larger projects where the client needs to be reassured you will stick to a particular budget.

Contracts

Whether you think you need a contract for a particular job really depends on the amount of work involved and the level to which you feel you need to be assured that it will continue. For a day or two's copywriting it is hardly worth the effort of getting a client to sign a contract. But if you are looking at a project that will provide a significant portion of your income, and for which you might have to turn down other work, you might well want to take the precaution of drawing up a contract.

Engagement contracts are available from industry bodies like the National Union of Journalists. Your client may have a standard contract they will use, although beware that the small print might not be in your favour. For a very large project, you might want to take on a lawyer specifically to draw up a contract that gives you a measure of protection.

In most cases, however, the written communication between you and your client, including briefs, proposals and quotations, would probably constitute enough of a contract to be enforceable by law.

> **If you are in any doubt about the integrity of the company you are dealing with, it is probably a good idea to set out any special terms and conditions in writing before you start the work.**

8. Ensuring Repeat Business

There is one sure-fire way of ensuring repeat business: do a good job the first time round. If a client likes your work, they will come back to you for more, and be happy to recommend your services to others. Your aim should be to provide a service that is so valuable, you become indispensable.

As part of this process, it helps to develop a sense of the kinds of pressures your client is working under. One of the best ways of securing future work is to make your client look good in front of their bosses. In practice, this means not fouling up: avoiding simple spelling and grammar mistakes, taking care to look out for corporate buzz words or taboo phrases; and generally making sure your copy will ring all the right bells with its intended audience.

> **Try to ensure every job meets and exceeds your clients' expectations and that your service is impeccably professional every time. It is a tall order, and you are unlikely to always get it right. But try hard enough and your efforts should pay off.**

Know your limits!

Finally, be aware that it can sometimes pay to stay away from areas where you are not sure of your abilities. One poorly executed piece of work can be enough for a client to lose confidence in you. If you really fancy trying your hand at a type of job you have never done before, it might be best to make your client fully aware that this is new territory for you and, if they still want to go ahead, agree to do the work at a discount or waive all payment unless they are completely satisfied, so they do not feel they are taking a risk.

7

Getting Help

1. Don't Be Alarmed!

I have called this chapter Getting Help as a bit of a catch-all for some non-basic areas you might come across in the course of running your business, not because things are likely to go wrong. Thankfully, although copywriting can make an important contribution to an organisation's image and marketing success, it is rarely a matter of life-or-death importance and you are unlikely to get sued, lynched or otherwise persecuted if you foul up.

Usually, the worst that can happen in this line of business is that you miss a deadline or submit terrible copy for a really important project, in which case the client will (quite rightly, in my opinion) refuse to pay you and choose never to work with you again. Provided you are a competent writer and maintain at least a semblance of professionalism, you can generally avoid such situations.

Nevertheless, there are likely to be times when you will find it useful to seek help from other individuals and organisations. Here are some of the more obvious ones.

2. Lawyers and Legal Matters

In all the time I have been running my own business I have never needed to consult a lawyer and I sincerely hope things stay that way. Having said that, I can think of at least three situations in which legal help can be useful if not indispensable:

◆ If you are setting up a company or a partnership, rather than acting as a sole trader, it would probably be a good idea to get a lawyer involved in drawing up documents like employment contracts, partnership agreements and terms of engagement for clients.

◆ If you win a really important piece of work (one that is likely to provide most of your income for some time, for example), it would be useful to get a lawyer to draw up a contract for your client to sign, or look over any contracts provided by the client, to make sure that your position is safeguarded as far as possible if things go wrong.

◆ If your business involves publishing rather than simply working for publishers (for example if you produce a newsletter or website for general consumption), then you should have access to a lawyer who can make sure you will not fall foul of libel laws. (Many publishers have their own in-house legal person or team to take care of this.)

> **Whatever your requirement, you will probably need to find a legal expert with some degree of specialisation (particularly in the case of libel law) and you should ask around to see if your business contacts can recommend someone appropriate.**

3. Professional Bodies

The main professional bodies in the creative, media and marketing sectors, such as the Advertising Association (AA), the Direct Marketing Association (DMA) or the Public Relations Consultants Association (PRCA), tend to be geared towards agencies rather than individuals. As a result, membership of one or another of them is unlikely to be very worthwhile unless you are running a substantial business and/or have strong links with a particular sector, such as advertising.

There are exceptions to this. The National Union of Journalists (NUJ) and Institute of Copywriting, for example, both have more to offer freelances, probably in recognition of the greater number of people who go it alone in these fields. Even so, this does not necessarily mean that it will benefit you much to join them. The points to weigh up when considering membership of a professional body are:

◆ How much does it cost?

◆ Are you likely to get work, through referrals or introductions, if you join?

◆ Will clients be more likely to take you on if you are a member, or refuse your services if you are not?

◆ Does the organisation offer fringe benefits, such as reduced insurance cover, that offset the membership fee?

◆ Will the organisation's events help you network or give you access to expertise that you can draw on in your line of business?

◆ Will membership give you access to training or information that will be of benefit to you?

If in doubt, it might be worth talking to members to find out whether they think it is worthwhile. Some further points to bear in mind are:

◆ Membership of a professional body is not essential for running a successful copywriting business.

◆ Some professional bodies can be little more than old boys' clubs.

◆ If most of your copywriting work is within a particular industry, such as technology, you might get better value, both in terms of contacts and access to knowledge, from joining a relevant body in that industry.

◆ Many of the larger professional bodies will provide free information and advice to non-members.

There are contact details for professional bodies in the creative, media and marketing industries at the back of this book.

Is it worth becoming a member of a union?

The only properly unionised industry related to copywriting is journalism. If you do a lot of journalistic writing, it may well be worth becoming a member of the NUJ or a similar union, if for no other reason than your membership card will act as valid press identification and enable you to get into events and briefings you might not be admitted to otherwise. You will also, of course, have access to many other services, such as legal advice.

4. Working With Other Freelancers

When running your own business, the name of the game is usually to try to keep as much work as possible to yourself. There may be occasions, however, when you are faced with a project of such scope or complexity that it is worth bringing in other freelancers to help you out.

It may be that you are simply farming out a large piece of copywriting work, or that you are entrusted with a more complicated project, such as developing a magazine or a website, and need to bring in specialist help in the form of designers, photographers and so on.

This is where a network of business associates, if you have one, can really come into its own. When working on a large project, particularly if you have overall responsibility, it helps to be able to rely on people whose abilities you trust and perhaps with whom you have worked before.

If you do not know of anyone first-hand, it might be worth asking around business contacts and friends before resorting to non-recommended sources such as you might find advertised in industry magazines or on the internet. Alternatively, your client might be able to suggest someone they have worked with before.

Assembling and working with a 'virtual team' can be very satisfying if you usually work alone, and can theoretically give you access to much larger contracts. Another attraction is that teams can be assembled and disbanded as and when needed, much more flexibly than if you were employing people directly.

How you split the rewards will depend on the nature of the work and the makeup of the team. In some cases it may be easiest for you to invoice the client for the entire project and then pay your associates at an agreed rate. In other instances it might work out better for them all to be paid directly by the client. If you have any say in the matter, try to pick a method that involves the least risk to your business and ensures the quickest possible payment.

> **If you frequently give or receive work from a network of contacts, you might want to consider an informal new business reward scheme, where, for example, each person gives a small percentage of the fees they earn from referred jobs back to the referrer.**

5. Training

Do you need training to be a copywriter? It is difficult to say. Good copywriters tend to hone their skills in one of two major industries: advertising, where there is rarely any formal training to speak of, and journalism, where training is considered very important and is usually a key part of an apprenticeship. These two industries produce very different styles of writing, but with some fundamental similarities that are crucial to all types of copy, as we shall see later.

Ultimately, no amount of qualifications will outdo a strong client list and brilliant portfolio, so it is probably safe to say that training is not absolutely vital to being able to run a successful copywriting business. But when you are starting out some form of tuition, even if it is a one-day course or an evening class, can be immensely beneficial, if only in helping give you the confidence of knowing that your skills are up to scratch.

Sources of training are numerous and will depend on how much time and money you have to spend and what kind of writing you are interested in learning about. From personal experience, I can recommend the Periodical Publishing Association's courses to those who want to brush up on their journalistic skills. Other courses may be less useful; if possible, I would advise trying to speak to someone who has been on the course before you commit to going on it yourself.

Also bear in mind that it is not just training in writing skills that can benefit your business. A one day course on Microsoft Excel, for example, might pay dividends in helping you improve your ability to do your accounts. It is important to weigh up, however, the benefits of training yourself up to do new tasks compared with simply buying in the skills you need to do the job. Going on a web design course, for example, might be great fun, but in the long run you might find that it is quicker and cheaper to get someone else to build the websites for which you are writing copy.

A list of all possible sources of training is beyond the scope of this book. To find out more, I would recommend starting with some of the industry bodies listed under Sources and References at the back of the book, or asking work contacts to see what they recommend.

6. Finding Information

Being able to dig out information and present it succinctly is a valuable skill, as a successful copywriter often has to do a lot of research – frequently without many of the resources available to those working in large organisations.

Areas where you might need specialist information can range from material for particular client projects to your own plans for your business. If most of your work is within a particular sector, it is likely you will pick up a lot of background knowledge by a process of osmosis. In other cases, though, you will need to resort to desk research.

Nowadays the internet is a first port of call in any fact-finding mission and if you are not already familiar with the way different search engines work, it is worth spending some time getting to know them and learning the basics, such as how to narrow down searches by putting phrases in inverted comas. The services that I use most often are:

◆ Google – probably the quickest and easiest to use. The image search is very useful for pictures if you are presenting rough creative ideas.

◆ Yahoo! – use its directories for hunting down territory-specific information, such as the *Yellow Pages* in Paris.

◆ UKPlus – for UK-based sites only.

◆ Ask – for information that cannot be found by a simple keyword search, such as 'What is the cost of living in different countries around the world?'

The addresses for all these sites are listed at the back of this book. Other useful websites include (in no particular order):

◆ Companies House – for basic information on UK companies.

◆ BT.com – for online directory enquiries.

◆ Whatis.com – an online dictionary of technical abbreviations, essential for technology writers.

◆ Altavista translations – for help with foreign language source material.

◆ BBC.co.uk – for breaking news.

◆ Dictionary.com – for word definitions.

In addition, every industry has key information sources you will want to tap into if they relate to your clients. If you work on a lot of technology projects, for example, you will probably want to subscribe to Silicon.com and TheRegister.co.uk; in accounting, AccountingWeb.co.uk and AccountancyAge.co.uk; and so on.

Part Two
YOUR WRITING

8

Delivering Great Copy

1. What Makes Great Copy?

This is the most important chapter in the book. It is about what makes great copy. Without the skills outlined in this chapter, no matter how much business acumen you have, the chances are you will not make a great success of copywriting. *With* these skills you will already have the basics you need to write any style of copy, although the chapters that follow may help give you some pointers on the style and approach needed for particular types of projects.

If you are expecting me to outline some secret winning formula, however, prepare to be disappointed. There is a winning formula, but it is far from secret. The rules you need to follow can be found all around you, in conversations in the pub, jokes on the internet and even Hollywood movies.

What all these have in common is that they are capable of engaging you and commanding your full attention, at least for a while. This is exactly what you, as a copywriter, need to be able to do – with any audience.

But how? What follows are a few simple rules of thumb that apply to all forms of effective communication. In a nutshell, all you need to do to write great copy is to keep it:

◆ short

◆ simple

◆ interesting

◆ relevant

◆ active and

◆ honest.

2. Keep It Short

It is quite common to have a lot to say, but most people do not have much time to listen – or read. So the first rule of copywriting is: keep it short. Remember that you are not a novelist; your audience is not asking you to give them something to read on the beach. Instead, think of your copy as a journey that the reader has to undertake to arrive at the message you are trying to pass on. No matter how interesting (and it *should* be interesting), your readers will want to get to the end in the quickest possible time, so help them by providing the most direct route. Get rid of any detours and use short cuts where possible.

The 'keep it short' rule applies to words, sentences and entire texts. In your copy, every word should count. There should be no padding, no dross. With everything you write, look to see if you can cut the number of words you use and still retain meaning. Do this once, twice, as many times as you can. What you will find is that every time you cut words, your message becomes more direct and more powerful, because you are stripping away excess to reveal the core of what you want to say.

Let's take an example. Here is a fairly straightforward commercial message:

'The reason why you should buy my book, which is called *How to Set Up a Freelance Writing Business*, is that it will help you to become a better writer and make more money.'

At 34 words, you might think this is pretty succinct. But watch:

'The reason you should buy my book, *How to Set Up a Freelance Writing Business*, is it will help you to become a better writer and make more money.'

We have taken out five words without changing the meaning of the sentence at all. What were those words doing? Just taking up space and time – and preventing the reader from progressing quickly onto the next important point. If you look carefully at any text, you will usually find there are words that simply sit around without contributing to the meaning of sentences. The word 'that' is a good example; it can usually be replaced by 'which', or taken out altogether.

Now let's see if we can cut away even more. How about:

'Buy my book, *How to Set Up a Freelance Writing Business* – it will help you to become a better writer and make more money.' (24 words)

Or even:

'Buy my book, become a better writer and make more money.' (11 words)

Notice how each time words are taken away, the message becomes more direct and thus more powerful. How far can we go with this process? The core message in this example might simply be: *'Buy my book'* – just three words, or less than nine per cent of the original sentence.

Don't just keep sentences short. Try to break up long paragraphs and words, too. Your aim should always be to minimise the number of syllables, or even letters, in your text. If in doubt, it is preferable to have a string of short words than a single long word. Better still, break up your long words and then rearrange each sentence so you get rid of some of the shorter words you have just created.

Watch out for unnecessary punctuation, too. In essence, if punctuation marks can be taken out of a sentence without changing its meaning or making it more difficult to understand, then get rid of them. Consider the following:

'Chief executive, Alan X, says: . . .'

And:

'Chief executive Alan X says: . . .'

Notice how the commas in the first line are not adding any information or clarification to the sentence. So they have to go. Notice also, however, that the commas would be justified if Alan X's name were being mentioned in a subordinate clause, as in:

'Company Y's chief executive, Alan X, says: . . .'

In a similar vein, leave full stops out of common abbreviations like 'Mr' or 'mph'.

How long should sentences be?

As a general rule, unless you are writing for a particularly highbrow audience, no sentence of commercial copy has any right to be much longer than about 50 words. For an intro, the first line of your text, you need to hook the reader with a short, sharp statement, so try to stick to 25 words or fewer. Keeping to these word counts will make your text easier to read. It will help you in other ways, too, for example in forcing you to clarify what you are trying to say and making you break your message down into small, bite-sized chunks of information.

Note that these word counts are for guidance only and will depend on the exact project you are working on. Be particularly wary of long sentences (and paragraphs) if you are writing for electronic media (because it is difficult to scan long lines of text on a screen) or direct mail. For advertising, where your intro is usually a headline, 25 words of copy is far too much. Aim for a dozen words maximum in your headline but remember the name of the game is to write as little, rather than as much, as possible. If you can summarise your ad in one word of copy, then do it.

3. Keep It Simple

Notice how the paring-down process we used in the example above helped simplify what we were trying to say. Towards the end it becomes clear that the text contains a number of distinct messages:

'Buy my book.'

'Become a better writer.'

'And make more money.'

Breaking down a text into simple messages like this is another way of improving the readability and power of your copy. Once again, remember that you are not out to wow readers with your literary prowess, but to give them an unequivocal motive to take some form of action. Highlight each point clearly and concisely, so the reader is left in no doubt about what you are saying.

Presenting your argument one point at a time can be important in helping you work out the structure of your text. If you are writing a feature, for example, it is worth setting out all the points in the argument you want to make and then writing a paragraph on each; as you go along you will be able to see where it would make sense to include quotes, statistics and so on.

The 'keep it simple' rule applies to different types of project in the same way as sentence length. Keep things *very* simple in texts for electronic, broadcast and tabloid media, advertising and direct mail. If you are in any doubt as to how you should simplify a complicated argument, a good tip is to pick up a tabloid newspaper and see how they have treated similar subjects.

Finally, presenting your argument in simple terms is useful in helping you work out the order of your messages – and, crucially, what should be the first thing you can say that will capture the reader's attention.

The Fog Index

If you are worried about the readability of your copy, you can use a measure called the Fog Index to assess whether you need to simplify it. The Fog Index quantifies how complicated a text is in terms of the number of years of schooling required to understand it. This is how you use it:

◆ Work out the average number of words per sentence in your text. You can do this by dividing the number of words by the number of sentences in a couple of paragraphs. Independent clauses (such as 'The time for words is over; now, action is needed') count as separate sentences.

◆ Count up the number of words in the same section of text that have three syllables or more, ignoring proper names.

◆ Add the two figures and then multiply the sum by 0.4 to get your Fog Index.

The Fog Index of the bullet points above works out at about ten, which is more or less the same as text in *Time, Newsweek* or the *Wall Street Journal*. Such a score is alright for educated audiences (like the anticipated readership of this book), but far too high for mass-market copy. Tabloid newspapers (and, interestingly, great works like the Bible and Shakespeare's plays) tend to have Fog Indexes of almost half that level. And if your copy has a Fog Index of more than about 12, it is probably too complicated for most people to read easily.

If you use a word processor to produce copy, it will probably have other statistics that can help you gauge readability. Microsoft Word, for example, has two readability indices (which can be switched on via the 'Options' panel under 'Tools'):

♦ **Flesch Reading Ease**, which ranges from zero to 100, with higher numbers indicating greater readability. Average texts should score between 60 and 70.

♦ **Flesch-Kincaid Grade Level**, which indicates readability in terms of US grade-school levels; anything above eighth grade would be considered of below-average readability.

4. Keep It Interesting

Although we have worked out that the key message (or, if you like, the desired outcome) in our earlier example is *'Buy my book'*, this does not mean it is the message that is most likely to get the reader to act in the way we want them to. I would expect you to have done so because, as someone who has, presumably, bought my book, you wanted to improve your writing skills or start your own business (or something else), but not because someone had told you to.

When faced with commercial communications, people are often much more likely to act if you talk to them about an idea (wealth, for example, or expertise) rather than a physical object (like a book). This is a technique which has been used by sales people for decades. In *How to Win Customers*, first published in 1957, ace salesman Heinz M. Goldmann writes:

> 'What you sell is never a product as such, but the idea behind the product – that is, the role played by that product in satisfying a customer's needs. The product is a means, not an end.'

Nowadays, the theory still holds true. In marketing it tends to be embodied in the phrase '*talk benefits, not features*'; in other words, what will grab the reader is an explanation of what a product or service can do rather than how it works. Nevertheless it is still amazing how often companies insist on talking about the features of their products in their commercial communications.

I am going to labour this point, because it is important. *People are not interested in what a product or service can do.* They are interested in what it can do *for them*. Whenever you have to write about something, don't think about what it is or does; think about what it means. Take a new computer, for example. You could talk about how it has a screen layout that makes it user-friendly; how even non-technical people could find it easy to work with. These things might be very important as far as your client is concerned, because, after all, they have spent a good deal of time, effort and money coming up with these features. But such messages are likely to be trivial to the average buyer. What interests the consumer is what these features might mean to their lives.

In the 80s, Apple Computer adopted this approach to launch its Macintosh machine. The advertising campaign it used, directed by Ridley Scott, did not feature a single shot of the product – or even a mention of what it could do. Instead it showed a character rebelling against an Orwellian society. In the consumer's mind, the Macintosh was thus powerfully linked to the concept of freedom. This positioning ultimately may have helped Apple become the preferred computer for creative professionals the world over. In the same way today, Volkswagen's award-winning advertising rarely makes a big deal about the cars it promotes, but instead focuses on ideas like security, enjoyment or roominess.

What this illustrates about the 'benefits, not features' approach is that it is ultimately designed to elicit an emotional, rather than rational, response from the audience. And this is largely what drives purchase behaviour. This response can be as subtle as presenting a product or service in terms that make it 'feel right' to the customer; hence why large organisations spend millions of pounds on brand advertising campaigns that are solely about making particular consumer groups feel an affinity with their name. As a copywriter, your job is to convince your audience; but you will do that only if you can make it feel something.

5. Keep It Relevant

Making your copy interesting is all well and good, but you also have to remember that different things appeal to different people. So the first question you have to ask yourself with any copywriting project is: who am I writing for?

In virtually all assignments, you will find there are usually two or more distinct audiences. First there is the ultimate audience, the one your client is trying to reach. This may be consumers, business people or some sector of society; youth, for example, or professional women, or members of the press. If the ultimate audience is not clear from your client's brief, then make sure you establish what it is before you get to work. And if you are not personally acquainted with the ultimate audience, find out as much as possible about them, both from your client and from other sources. You need to find out what drives these people and what messages they will respond to, so that your copy will grab their attention.

As well as being relevant to your ultimate audience in content, your copy needs to be relevant in tone. Youth audiences are unlikely to respond to corporate speak, for example. But beware of overdoing it if you are not familiar with the language of a particular group or you could end up alienating the audience you are trying to get through to. If in doubt, stick to simple, straightforward words and phrases as these make sense in any dialect.

Besides your ultimate audience (and there may be more than one of these), you also have to satisfy an immediate audience: your client. This means that your copy has to be consonant with your client's organisation and take account of its style and approach to communications. Again, if these are not outlined in your brief, it is worth querying your client on what they would and would not like to see in your text. Remember, also, that the ultimate audience is likely to have certain expectations about how they will be spoken to by your client's business.

It is probably obvious at this point that your immediate and ultimate audiences may have widely different expectations and requirements. In general, your job as a copywriter is to try as far as possible to steer your client towards using the language of the ultimate audience, as this is the approach that should achieve the best results.

However, you also need to be sensitive to your client's idiosyncrasies, particularly if these are imposed by some higher authority. It is usually possible to come to some form of compromise, but if you cannot reconcile the two types of content and tone then you really have only two options: resign the work or accept the client's point of view (with reservations, if necessary) and do it their way.

Which you choose is up to you but personally I favour the latter. You still get paid and many clients appreciate the effort that you put in on their behalf plus the fact that you understand the constraints they operate under.

A final point on how to keep your copy relevant to your readers: talk about them. When writing marketing copy, it is easy to say 'we do this', 'we do that'. Your client's readers, however, are in the main not interested in hearing about your client. So write text that says: 'we'll help *you* do this', '*you'll* do that'. As a basic rule of thumb, if your copy says 'you' more often than it says 'we', then you are talking in language that is likely to appeal to readers. Get into the habit of checking that this is always the case.

> **Keeping things short, simple, accurate and relevant is important in all types of copy and you should ensure that you apply these rules as second nature throughout your writing. The next two rules are also crucial, but their importance can vary according to the type of project you are working on.**

6. Keep It Active

Consider the following two sentences:

'Savings of £2 million a year have been generated by the new procedure.'

'The new procedure has generated savings of £2 million a year.'

Both say the same thing, but the second sentence uses an active rather than a passive voice. In the first instance, X *is done by* Y. In the second, Y *does* X. Notice the latter is shorter, simpler, more direct and more powerful. It is easy to write in the passive voice because it sounds more long-winded and 'authoritative'; as a result, it is commonly used in management documents and the like. This is not the way your copy should read. As I have already mentioned, when writing copy you are not trying to impress people with your wordiness, but attempting to grab their attention and get an emotional response from them that will drive them to act. Using the active voice will ensure your copy is unambiguous, direct and personal. There may be exceptions to this rule. If you are writing a report or a management document, you might feel justified in adopting a passive voice because it will result in language your audience will feel more at home with. Even so, I would probably argue that use of the active voice would still make your text more effective; try switching some of your sentences around to see how they read.

Using Anglo-Saxon

In a similar vein, Crawford Kilian, author of the excellent *Writing for the Web*, advocates using Anglo-Saxon root words rather than Latin root words where possible. His rationale is that the latter were introduced into the English language by the Roman administration and in many cases replaced shorter, 'vulgar' Anglo-Saxon terms which are quicker and easier to read and carry a much higher emotional charge. To demonstrate how effective this technique is, consider the following Latin root words that I used on purpose in this paragraph – and their Anglo-Saxon counterparts:

Latin	*Anglo-Saxon*
• introduce	• bring in
• administration	• chiefs
• demonstrate	• show
• effective	• good
• consider	• look at

7. Keep It Honest

If you look carefully you might notice that all the points I have made so far
are in fact variations on a theme. They all refer to putting across a message
as directly and succinctly as possible. Such messages will be easier to
understand and therefore more transparent to the audience reading them.
Which brings us on to the final basic rule for great copy: honesty. Honesty
is crucial in copywriting because, quite simply, customers are unlikely to buy
from an organisation they do not trust. This lack of trust may be explicit in
the company's communications, for example through blatant over-claiming
in advertising. But it can also, very often, be implicit in the use of
long-winded language and technical jargon which appears to have little
substance. If customers cannot understand what a piece of copy is saying,
why should they trust the organisation it comes from? There is another
good reason to stick to honest, accurate text. In many areas of writing, such
as journalism or advertising, if you mislead your readers you can get into
serious legal trouble.

Accuracy of information

As a copywriter, it is your job to cram as much information as possible into
as few words as you can. That means you deal with a lot of information:
names, dates, quotations, figures, theories, concepts, assumptions and so on.
It is ultimately up to you to make sure they are all right. Someone else,
whether it is the legal department of a client company or the subeditor of a
magazine, may take some responsibility in checking what you have written,
but no customer of yours is going to thank you for handing in material that

is riddled with mistakes. So get used to questioning and checking every fact that goes into your copy. Also, do not assume that everything you read has been checked with the same diligence you should apply to your own copy. Much published information in newspapers, magazines and websites is notoriously inaccurate because the content is often generated at speed and with access to a limited number of sources. (It is sometimes said that information on the web is less trustworthy than that in the print media but my personal opinion is that the level of misreporting in both types is about the same. Online misinformation, however, can spread much more quickly and widely.)

Particular areas to watch out for (often because you may think you know what you are talking about when you do not) are:

◆ Place names (check against a good atlas).

◆ Name spellings (always check when you speak to someone and if in doubt then cross-reference your notes with published material, if available).

◆ Job titles (if in doubt, a phone call to a company switchboard can help).

◆ Company names (the phone book or the company's corporate website are good ways to cross-check these; and beware of style points, such as names that are written with a lower-case initial).

◆ Figures (if they are sums of money, always check the currency).

◆ Sources (always provide a reference to the original source of information if you can, even if it is simply 'research company X says'. On the web, you may be able to link directly to the source instead).

Accuracy extends to spelling and grammar, of course. While some people do not believe you should rely on automated spell checkers, they are at least useful for picking up the kind of obvious mistakes that can creep in when you are rushing to meet a deadline; just make sure you have your spell checker switched to the version of English that your audience will be reading in.

As for grammar, there is a case for doing away with as much spurious punctuation as possible (see above) but make sure your text does not become ambiguous in the process. The best option, as always, is to stick to short, simple sentences.

Accuracy versus interest

Since your copy is intended to grab a reader's interest, it is not unusual (particularly with dull subject matter) to come across a conflict between the truth and what you would *like* to say.

Much advertising seems to over-claim routinely (*'Our herbal remedy will change your life forever!'*) to the point where most audiences now recognise a level of poetic licence as an inherent feature of the medium. (In fact, as I will come back to in Chapter 10, around 70 per cent of people do not believe what adverts say at all.) Nevertheless, claims which are factually incorrect (for example, *'Our product is 20 per cent cheaper than our nearest competitor's'* – when it is not) can still land you in trouble. The smart copywriter will ignore the temptation to jazz up a product or service offering with fancy claims and, instead, look for something that will act as a unique selling point (USP, of which more in Chapter 10) for the target audience. Preferably, too, this will be linked to an emotional response rather than a feature of the product or service, which again lessens the potential for misrepresentation.

Sometimes it can be practically impossible to think of anything interesting to say about your client's product or service. If you are stuck in this situation, look again at what appeals to the target audience. After all, *someone* must be interested in buying what you have to sell. Think also about modifying your creative approach; could the message be jazzed up if it were delivered through a different medium, for example? However, if after much thought you cannot come up with anything truthful about a product or service that you believe will interest an audience, you might just be justified in advising your client to re-think how they want to go about promoting it.

Proofreading

The smallest mistakes are the easiest ones to make: writing 'an' instead of 'and', missing out a word, misspelling a name. These also tend to be the mistakes that are least likely to be picked up by a spell checker. Because most of your copy will be proofread by a client at some point or other, it can be tempting, particularly if you are working against the clock, to not worry too much about these tiny mistakes and to leave them for others to pick up. Do not be tempted.

Handing your client copy that is riddled with basic mistakes makes your work look sloppy and unprofessional. And your client will not necessarily pick up on all your small mistakes. Some of them may make it through to the final version, with embarrassing and potentially costly consequences. Proofread everything you do before you send it off. Some people believe it helps to print a hard copy, since mistakes can be easier to spot on paper, but even a quick scan of your copy on screen is better than nothing – and could well help you spot a howler in the nick of time.

Do not just limit your proofreading to your copy, either. Make sure you check everything from proposals to emails. Since your writing is your trade, you can be judged on every word you put down, and you should admit no errors.

> **I have to own up: I am a lousy proofreader. I am forever sending off material I have not checked and then wincing when I spot a hideous mistake in it. It is my big weakness as a copywriter. So now go on and write to tell me what errors you have found in this book . . .**

8. Finding Inspiration

Having stripped away your message to the bare bones of what you want to say, you may wonder whether there will be any room left for that wonderful creativity copywriters are supposed to possess. How are you going to impress your client (and their audience) if you are barred from finding space for that great turn of phrase or simile you had in mind? How are you going to apply your written powers of persuasion in an intro just 25 words long? And surely it is a waste to confine all the research you have done into a topic to just 200 words of copy?

If that is your thinking, then forget it. I bet your 'wonderfully creative' copy would have ended up sounding pompous and long-winded. Directness and simplicity are paths to creativity, not obstacles to it. Distilling your message to its essence will give you a clear insight into what you are really trying to say. Working out what is interesting and relevant to your audience will help you discover new ways of saying it. The process can be summarised as follows:

- What am I really trying to say? ('Buy my book.')

- Why is this relevant to my audience? (It isn't, unless they want to improve their writing skills and earn more money.)

- What can I say that will get them interested in the first place? ('Earn more through writing.')

If you know what you want to say but are really stuck for an original way to put it, here are some tips that might help throw up the headline or intro you are looking for.

- Narrow down your message to one or two key words and think about whether they have any connection or double meaning that might work in another context relevant to your audience.

- Ask yourself 'What if . . . ?' questions about your subject matter (for example: 'What if everyone was given a free product X?').

- Take a train of thought regarding your subject matter to its logical conclusion (for example: detergent X washes whiter than ever; so white your clothes might blind you; so you write: 'Optician's warning – buy sunglasses before use').

◆ Turn your argument on its head and think about the consequences of not using the products and services you are promoting. This technique has been used in marketing for generations, to create demand for goods that would probably be hard to justify otherwise. Think about why you buy toilet cleaner. Sure, it kills those nasty bugs which are supposed to live in your loo bowl. But how often do you touch your loo bowl anyway?

> **In many areas of writing, such as journalism, web copywriting or case study production, you should be able to pull out an interesting intro from your source material. While you are researching the subject, look out for unusual statistics, quotes or trends that you can use.**

9. How To Present Copy

There are no golden rules on how you should present your copy to your client. After all, what is important is what is said rather than what it looks like. Some obvious points to bear in mind, however, are:

◆ It is useful to include a header with information like the document title, draft number, date, approval stage and, if necessary, your contact details.

◆ Headlines, sub-headings and so on should be clearly identified as such with labels that will not be mistaken for part of the main text.

◆ Indicate where the text ends, in case part of it gets lost in faxing or printing.

◆ Include a word count if this is relevant to the job.

◆ Include page numbers on documents that are several pages long.

◆ On very large documents, such as proposals or website drafts, it is useful to have a contents page with links to headlines throughout the text.

◆ Give an idea of what any images or graphics being used with the text should look like, for example by including sketches or short descriptions.

9

Things to Watch Out For

1. Respect The Language

Beyond the basic rules of copywriting that I described in the previous chapter, there are many other points which you will need to bear in mind and which will become second nature as your experience grows. First among these is to get to know and respect the basic tool of your trade: the English language.

This quirky, difficult mishmash of words has evolved over the centuries into one of the foremost tongues on the planet, adopted by populations in virtually every continent and used by some of the finest writers in history. It dominates everything from the computer systems driving today's technology to the markets presiding over the global economy. Its spoken dialects are so diverse they can, on occasion, seem like languages in their own right; but the uniformity of written English ensures it can be understood the world over. You would think such a powerful force for communication would be sufficient for all its users in its present form; but sadly that does not appear to be the case.

Modern English is under attack from all quarters. Its assailants range from those who regularly breach basic rules of grammar because they know no better, to many who should know better yet persist in wantonly trying to twist the law of language in the mistaken belief that it will make them seem just that little bit smarter or more interesting. You will find out who I am talking about in just a minute. For the time being, though, pick up a dictionary and leaf through the rich variety of words and meanings therein. Grab a novel (preferably a good one) and see how the language is used to express complex ideas with clarity and precision. Then go out on the street and see if you can spot how many times this wonderful tool is being misused by ignoramuses or smartarses. Make sure you never join their ranks once you take up copywriting as your trade.

Written English, as is the case with most languages, is governed by a set of very simple rules. For example:

- Sentences start with a capital letter and end with a full stop.

- Elsewhere, capital letters are used for names.

- Sentences can be broken up using commas, colons, semi-colons, dashes or parentheses.

- If there is a direct quote in a sentence, this is enclosed in inverted commas.

- Apostrophes are used to indicate possessive words (except in the case of 'it') or contractions.

- Bold or italic type is usually used to provide emphasis, for example in headlines.

There are many more basic rules, of course, and they are all there for a good reason: they help the reader understand what is being said. Any deviation from them is likely to cause confusion and is therefore pointless and unnecessary. But it is easy to find examples of even the few rules above regularly being broken in the name of corporate communications. As a copywriter, you will undoubtedly find yourself being invited to participate in this process, usually under the guise of 'sticking to corporate guidelines'. While I am not suggesting you jack in the job at this point, it is worth resisting where possible and explaining to your client that the correct use of language can only enhance the value of their communications. Whatever you do, never feel tempted to misuse the language yourself unless there is a really good reason for doing so.

> **What follows is something of a rogues' gallery of common language abuse.**

2. Abbreviations

Most businesses operate in specialised fields filled with technical phrases that have been shortened to abbreviations. Some of these, such as 'CD' for 'compact disc', may be fairly well known to the general public. Most are not. My advice is to check whether any abbreviation you want to use has entered common usage by looking to see if it is listed in the dictionary. If not, assume your readers will be ignorant of its meaning. Do them a favour by spelling out what it stands for the first time you use it. Being aware of the exact meanings of common abbreviations can also help you stay clear of embarrassing mistakes such as 'PIN number'.

One area to be particularly wary of is technological abbreviations that have entered the mainstream. A good example is 'WAP'. This stands for wireless application protocol, a standard which allows mobile phones to receive internet content, but it is not likely to mean much to the person on the street even when spelt out. One option if you are writing to a general audience is to spell out the abbreviation and follow it with a brief description of what the technology does: 'a wireless application protocol mobile, which can receive internet content . . .' This is hardly succinct but it does, with any luck, leave the reader in no doubt as to what you are talking about. Other technological abbreviations, such as IP (for internet protocol) or SMS (short message service) are becoming more common as equipment based on them enters the mainstream. However, they have yet to attain the same currency as, say, 'IT', which can nowadays safely be used in its abbreviated form without danger of confusion.

Abbreviations are a particular problem for copywriters in internal communications, because each business not only uses standard trade jargon but also has its own shorthand for departments, processes, job titles and so on. The experienced writer may guess that RSM stands for 'regional sales manager' but other abbreviations can be completely baffling, and not just for outsiders. In one organisation I have come across, employees are handed a book (not a list) containing several hundred abbreviations that they might encounter. Clearly, in situations like this, it is safe to assume that even many long-standing employees may not have been able to digest every single acronym. It will be up to you to establish with the client which ones are likely to be widespread enough to warrant use without being spelt out.

> **Never write abbreviations such as 'e.g.' or 'etc.' as these make it look as if you cannot be bothered with the text. Instead use 'for example', 'for instance', 'and so on' or a similar phrase.**

3. Apostrophes

The rules governing the use of apostrophes are pretty simple. The apostrophe is used to denote possessiveness (as in *'John's plan'*) or the loss of letters when two words are contracted into one (as in *don't*). The only exception to this rule is 'it', which does not have an apostrophe in its possessive form ('its') so that it can be distinguished from the contraction of 'it is'. Nevertheless, for most people the use of the apostrophe seems about as difficult to grasp as the offside rule in soccer. Go to any high street (and many websites too, for that matter) and you will spot apostrophes being used willy-nilly just about anywhere, but particularly in plural forms.

These so-called grocers' apostrophes (named because the illiteracy of traders seems to be the main driving force behind them) lead to abominations like *potato's* instead of *potatoes* and are now so entrenched in common usage that there are even moves to accept them into the formal written language. A more insidious version of the problem occurs with plurals of acronyms: *CD's* is now so widely used as the plural for compact discs that most ordinary people would probably have to think twice before guessing the correct form.

The its/it's rule is also often a common source of problems for novice writers, as is the use of apostrophes in words ending in 's'. In the latter case, the best rule is simply to follow the spoken sound, as in *James's plan* and *two years' worth*. Generally, though:

◆ Try to avoid contractions where possible, to avoid confusion (exceptions are in direct quotes or where you need to save space, such as in website copy).

◆ Know the rules governing the use of apostrophes and the its/it's rule in particular.

◆ Beware that spell checkers will not necessarily pick up on apostrophe mistakes.

4. Capital Letters in Names

Capital letters are used at the start of sentences and to denote proper nouns, like Jason Deign. No problem with that. It is a convention which has helped generations of readers make sense of the texts they are reading. That was until the last decade or so, at least. Since then, a growing number of companies appear to have decided they could defy the laws of grammar and use a lower-case initial in their name, even when it started a sentence. This trend (whose followers I shall not name, but which include several large organisations you are very likely to have heard of) appears to been born out of re-branding exercises where businesses have invested a substantial amount of money in a name and logo and where the branding agency decides a lower case initial is an essential part of the new brand identity. Leaving aside the issue of whether a branding agency should dictate how the rest of the world uses the English language, I believe this practice is a pointless affectation on a number of levels:

◆ It impairs readability and understanding.

◆ It is almost impossible to maintain consistently in practice as most people (and word processing systems) will revert to using initial caps anyway.

◆ It assumes the company name and logo are the same, which is not the case. They are two separate elements of an organisation's brand identity.

Similarly annoying are companies that use odd combinations of lower and upper case letters in their names (easyJet, for example; why not Easyjet?). If you are working as a journalist, you will often find your publication's editorial guidelines are pretty strict on how these names should be written (and it is usually using the standard convention of an initial capital letter followed by lower case). If you are working for a company that has one of these names, you will probably have to stick to its corporate guidelines, but do not be afraid to ask.

Finally, if you are ever in a position to advise a business on how its name should be written, tell your client that anything other than the standard convention is only going to cause headaches. Even companies like BT and BAA, whose all-upper-case names are based on pre-privatisation acronyms, find they are still regularly referred to in the press by their former labels (British Telecom and British Airports Authority, respectively).

> **You have probably noticed that I have used a lower case 'i' for 'internet' and lower case 'w' for 'web' throughout this book. This was a conscious decision based on the fact that, at the time of writing, these words were becoming so frequently used that they appeared to be taking on the status of common nouns. As a writer, you need to be sensitive to such changes in the language, although in general I would recommend caution in adopting new modes of spelling or punctuation.**

5. Collective Nouns

Companies and other commercial organisations are single entities, yet a common mistake in corporate communications is for businesses to refer to themselves in the plural, as in: 'Bloggs & Co are proud to present a new range of lawnmowers . . .'

The same goes for departments, teams and other business units. The correct use should be: 'Marketing *is* recruiting four new members of staff'; 'The project team *is* about to make an important announcement'. Note, however, that: '*Members* of the project team *are* expecting an important announcement.'

Exceptions to this rule are the police and sports teams.

6. Exclamation Marks

The exclamation mark is an almost completely spurious piece of punctuation. Its purpose in normal writing is to attract attention to a statement.

But in commercial texts, where every line is supposed to deliver a simple, clear statement, adding exclamation marks should be unnecessary. Either your line of copy will stand up in its own right, or not at all. If you add exclamations, you will probably succeed only in making your writing look tacky.

Following a line with several exclamation marks in a row is the ultimate sign of shoddy writing, which is probably why the ploy appeals so much to companies that send out junk mail.

7. Jargon

Whatever field of industry you end up writing for, sooner or later you will come up against jargon: a whole set of words and phrases that have either been misappropriated or completely made up by a group of users. Marketing types, for example, may be heard to utter phrases such as 'above the line', 'agency-side' or 'marcomms'. Technology bods will talk about 'platforms', 'interoperability' and 'resilience'. Jargon tends to be loved by those in the know because they are liable to believe it helps give them an air of informed superiority. For those outside this cosy industry circle, jargon usually comes across as meaningless waffle – which is why copywriters should try to avoid it at all costs. Jargon usually breaks down into made-up words and misused words. I will give an example of each to illustrate what you should look out for.

Made-up words

Managers are fond of taking nouns and turning them into verbs. Thus, to 'provide an incentive' becomes 'incentivise'. Having come up with a completely new word, there is little to stop them going further; hence the process of 'giving incentives' becomes 'incentivisation'. Such terms may impress the board but are unlikely to do much for the business's communications generally. As mentioned above, audiences will tend to treat with suspicion any communication that is couched in terms they cannot understand easily. Filling a text with long-winded, obviously made-up words like 'incentivisation' is just asking for trouble.

Misused words

Every now and then an industry feels it does not have enough perfectly good words of its own and steals a word from elsewhere. A classic example of this, and one of my personal bugbears, is the word 'solution'.

A quick search for this word on the reference site Dictionary.com reveals that, according to *Webster's*, 'solution' means:

1. The act of separating the parts of any body, or the condition of undergoing a separation of parts; disruption; breach.
2. The act of solving, or the state of being solved; the disentanglement of any intricate problem or difficult question; explanation; clearing up; used especially in mathematics, either of the process of solving an equation or problem, or the result of the process.
3. The state of being dissolved or disintegrated; resolution; disintegration.
4. The act or process by which a body (whether solid, liquid, or gaseous) is absorbed into a liquid, and, remaining or becoming fluid, is diffused throughout the solvent; also, the product resulting from such absorption.
5. Release; deliverance; discharge.
6. (a) The termination of a disease; resolution. (b) A crisis. (c) A liquid medicine or preparation (usually aqueous) in which the solid ingredients are wholly soluble.

There is no mention here (or in any other standard dictionary) of the word 'solution' meaning anything to do with a collection of software and hardware systems put together by a technology company.

Yet take a look at any text from any high-tech firm and you will see it is littered with references to the 'solutions' it offers its clients. What they are talking about is probably best illustrated by another entry in Dictionary.com, from The Free On-line Dictionary of Computing, by Denis Howe:

> **Solution** <jargon> A marketroid term for something he wants to sell you without bothering you with the often dizzying distinctions between hardware, software, services, applications, file formats, companies, brand names and operating systems; 'Flash is a perfect image-streaming solution.' 'What is it?' 'Um . . . about a thousand dollars.'

This insidious misuse of the word is so widespread that it has even been embraced by other industries (so, for example, cleaning services have become cleaning solutions) and incorporated into trading names (Bloggs & Co Cleaning Solutions).

Furthermore, people I have spoken to in technology companies are often genuinely surprised that anyone would not know what a 'solution' is in the context of computer systems, although they themselves are often stumped when pushed for a definition. The reality is that 'solution' is a non-word that does the industry no favours because it provides no information whatsoever on what businesses in the sector can offer to their clients.

8. Repetition

Using the same word or phrase over and over again is lazy and makes for boring reading. Vary your language as much as possible and try not to use long words or phrases twice in the same paragraph. If you cannot avoid repetition, then consider breaking the paragraph in two. It is handy to have a thesaurus to hand at all times so you can talk about the same thing in a variety of ways. For example, rather than saying 'company' all the time, try 'organisation', 'business', 'corporation' and so on.

9. Use of Italics, Bold or Upper Case Type

Italic, bold and upper case typefaces are usually reserved for words that need special emphasis, but should be used with extreme caution because they impair reading. Even in headlines, using upper case type can slow down the brain's ability to process information. This is because the brain scans lines of text by picking up on letters that stick out from the rest; in upper case text, all letters are the same height, so this information is lost.

To demonstrate this effect, here are two lines of text with only the top half showing. Which can you read more clearly from a distance?

Let's see if you can read this

OK, NOW TRY WITH THIS

You need to pay particular attention to the use of different typefaces when writing copy for the web. Words should never be underlined as this is standard online convention for a link to another page, so it will confuse readers. On the other hand, picking out intros and salient paragraphs in bold or italic type can actually improve readability on screen by giving the eye reference points to follow, particularly when scrolling down pages. However, different devices will display text in different ways, so you have to allow for the fact that your italicised emphasis might not show up in a text message.

> **In general, stick to short, simple copy and let the words speak for themselves so you do not have to resort to typography to make your point.**

10. Words To Watch Out For

The following are culled from a variety of sources and form the basis for many style guides I have put together. Some of the rules may vary slightly from one client to another; if in doubt, ask for a copy of the corporate guidelines or consult with your client.

◆ Affect/effect – the first means to influence, the second means to cause or achieve (as a verb), or result (as a noun).

◆ Afterwards – with an 's'.

◆ Alternative – there can be only two of these; otherwise they would be options or choices.

◆ Assure/ensure/insure – the first is to guard against certain risks (hence life assurance), the second is to make certain and the third is to guard against uncertain risks (hence fire insurance).

◆ Between – convention is 'between x and y', not 'between x-y'.

◆ Buy-out, buy out – the first is the noun, second the verb.

◆ Chairman – also applies to women as a job title.

◆ Close – use in preference to 'close down'.

◆ Complement/compliment – the first means to make up (a whole), the second is to praise.

◆ Cut – use in preference to 'cut back' (verb) or 'cutback' (noun).

◆ Despatch/dispatch – the first is a noun, the second is a verb.

◆ High street – lower case unless it refers to an address.

◆ Like – try not to use in place of 'such as'.

◆ Per annum – use 'a year' instead.

◆ Programme/program – the latter is an American spelling that in UK English applies only to computer software.

◆ Shut – use in preference to 'shut down'.

◆ UK – abbreviation for England, Wales, Scotland and Northern Ireland. Note that 'Great Britain' includes only the first three, while 'British Isles' is all of Great Britain and Ireland.

◆ While – preferred to 'whilst'.

11. US or UK English?

If you are working for a multinational organisation, or for the web, it is likely your copy will be seen by a high proportion of overseas readers, which in turn may mean you have to use US rather than UK English. There is no hard and fast rule over which version should take precedence, but in general:

◆ If your copy will be read predominantly by people in the UK, Europe, Middle East or Africa, stick to UK English.

◆ If your copy will be read predominantly by people in North or South America, use US English.

Asia is a bit more complicated. Some countries, such as India or Nepal, will probably favour UK English while Pacific Rim nations may be more at home with American. If in doubt, it is probably best to use the latter. Australians, of course, have their own particular uses of the language.

> **If you are writing in US English, do not forget that it is not just the spellings of words that are different; the meanings can change, too. Hence what Americans call a 'trolley' is a tram to Europeans, while a shopping trolley is known as a 'cart' in the United States.**

12. Avoid Clichés

A final point which should hardly need labouring: filling your copy with clichés is hardly going to win you much credit for originality or effort. Beware of buzzwords that can seem great one month but hackneyed the next. Among others, the following words and phrases have become virtually meaningless by overuse online and in the media. They are best avoided if possible:

access (as a verb)	and more	anticipate
at this moment in time	basically	biggest
boom	burgeoning	catastrophic
clearly	crucial	currently
cutbacks	cutting-edge	delighted
dramatic	effectively	enhanced
essentially	furthermore	giant
having said that	here is	hike (as in prices)
hopefully	hot	however
hugely influential	influential	circles
input	ironically	just
largest	leading	leading-edge
lion's share	literally	major
massive	meaningful	moreover
naturally	now	of course
offered	panic	per annum
persons	present	presently
pressure (as a verb)	pressurise	prestigious
quick to point out	raft	rocketed
slash	slump	sources
such as	swath	tasked with
tight-lipped	tranche	unique
unprecedented	very	well-informed.

This chapter and the preceding one have covered fundamentals that apply to any form of copywriting. What follows next are chapters on the major disciplines you are likely to come across in the course of running your business.

10

Writing for Advertising

1. Before We Start

Advertising is arguably the most coveted field of copywriting and undoubtedly one of the most written about. If you are set on getting into advertising and want to do it above all else, there are plenty of books written by grand masters in the field that will help you along (although you will still probably need massive doses of talent, application and luck). What follows is therefore *not* a definitive guide for the would-be advertising professional, but some tips and hints for general copywriters who may find themselves from time to time faced with having to put together ads as part of their wider writing work.

2. What Does Advertising Do?

Most people would probably assume that advertising helps sell products. This is true, but the process by which it does so is not always straightforward; or else why, for example, would companies that sell only very expensive computing or network equipment advertise on the telly (and many do), when the vast majority of the people who will see the commercials will probably not even understand what a router or server does, let alone want to buy one? The reason is that sales can be improved in two ways, with correspondingly different advertising approaches.

Promotional advertising

Promotional advertising is a direct attempt to get customers to purchase: 'Sale ends this week' or 'Buy one get one free', for example. It was this kind of blunt sales message that gave birth to advertising.

Promotional advertising today is still largely about raising awareness of a special offer or product that will have an appeal to a particular audience. In this sense, it can sometimes act more as a public information service than a sales tool. There is in fact some evidence to suggest that this is how advertising works – by providing raw information to customers who then base their buying behaviour on other, more subtle factors.

It is interesting to note that the interactive medium was dominated early on by increasingly obtrusive promotional ads. In recent years, however, there has been a growing awareness of the benefits of another form of advertising online: one that concentrates on the brand.

Brand advertising

One of these 'more subtle factors' is how the consumer feels about the company whose products they are buying. As I pointed out in Chapter 9, buying decisions are based as much on emotions as they are on rational thought. What this means in practice is that, all other things being equal, people are more likely to buy goods from companies they feel an affinity with. It is obviously very difficult for a consumer to get enough information to make a considered judgement on every business they interact with, so this affinity is usually based on the kind of evaluation we all carry out when meeting other people for the first time.

When you meet someone, you form an idea of them based on their appearance, on what they say and, over time, what they do. If their appearance, thoughts and actions mirror yours closely, you are likely to have a high degree of affinity with them. (Note how, when you are introduced to someone, you will usually try to find out what they do, where they come from and so on, in order to establish common ground.)

With businesses, this combination of image, communication and action is effectively what is known as the 'brand'. As with people, businesses can create a high degree of initial affinity with their customers through image and communications alone. Much of the effort in modern-day businesses is devoted to creating brands rather than manufacturing, a process documented in Naomi Klein's best-selling book *No Logo*, among others. Some companies, such as Nike, for example, even attribute most of their success to this shift. But ultimately, this 'brand value' will be lost if the actions of the business do not measure up to what it says.

This has not stopped advertisers from cottoning on to the fact that commercials can have a profound effect on the way people feel about their businesses. Hence brand advertising: a whole area of communications that is not about selling *per se*, but rather about the philosophies and values that the advertiser wants its customers to believe it embraces. The Apple computer ad discussed in Chapter 8, for example, is an excellent example of brand advertising, and nowadays this type of communication increasingly dominates the market.

By now you may have realised that brand and promotional advertising can work together to great effect, with the former creating the empathy that will attract customers to a company and the latter providing information that can act as a trigger to generate sales. When you take on ad copywriting work it is important for you to establish what kind of advertising your client wants as this will affect your approach. It is also important to point out that a single commercial can act on both a brand and a promotional level.

Brand positioning

Advertising can help link a brand to a set of attributes in the mind of the consumer, a process called brand positioning. Car brands provide an excellent example of this in action. Despite the fact that most cars look pretty similar these days, and are built to very similar standards, as far as the public is concerned Volvo stands for 'safe' (or, latterly, 'safe but quite racy'), Volkswagen stands for 'reliable', Land Rover stands for 'rugged' and so on. It could be argued that most of the sales of modern cars (and indeed of many other goods) are dependent on the attributes attached to the product through brand positioning.

3. Using Creativity To Sell

In recent years advertising has grown to fill almost every part of our environment. It pervades our screens, our landscape, our music, our clothing and much else besides. The arrival of so-called ambient media around two decades or so ago has enabled advertising to leap from its traditional haunts, such as television or billboards, to places as diverse as bus tickets, car park barriers and even dairy cows. It goes without saying that the profusion of commercial messages around us is such that an average person can expect to be bombarded by hundreds, if not thousands, of ads a day.

The net effect on us as consumers is that we tend to filter out advertising. Not entirely, though. Studies show people pick up a lot of their product information from advertising and will even make purchasing decisions based on how a brand markets itself through the media, despite the fact that they generally do not believe the claims of advertisers. The marketing researchers John E. Calfee and Debra Jones Ringold found that a constant 70 per cent or so of the population around the world believes that advertising is a useful source of information; the same as the proportion of people who say advertising claims cannot be believed (for more, see Calfee's excellent book *Fear of Persuasion*, published by Agora). Sadly for advertisers, the exact triggers that lead people to pick up on commercials are less clear. Hence the famous quote variously attributed to Lord Leverhulme, Frank W. Woolworth, John Wanamaker and others: 'I know half the money I spend on advertising is wasted. The trouble is I don't know which half.'

Nevertheless, the sheer amount of advertising that now bombards us means that it can be very difficult for a particular message to stand out.

This has led advertisers (and their agencies) to wage a war of one-upmanship with each other, boosting the cost and sophistication of commercials almost every year. While creativity is often seen as the key to success in this struggle, in reality what counts is an ability to understand the target market and work out what makes it tick.

The first thing the copywriter needs to do in devising a campaign is to work out what the client's product, service or brand means to real people. *Then* the creative process begins. Perhaps more than any other copywriting discipline, advertising relies on creative talents to get its message across. The reason is simple. Ads are ten a penny and people do not go looking for them. Most advertising is ignored. So to have any impact at all, an ad needs to get noticed then create an emotional response in its target audience.

Bear in mind that what works for one audience may not (or probably won't) be appropriate to another. One of my favourite poster ads from the 1990s, for a Japanese brand of beer, got slated in the press by a marketing head who could not understand the point of the creative. He was evidently not part of the target market. I evidently was, since I saw the ad, I liked it, and I bought the product.

> **Your task as a copywriter is to create an emotional bond between the brand you are promoting and its customers. So first of all, you need to understand what motivates those customers.**

Get to the point

Once you have worked out what will appeal to the target audience, get it across in as few words as possible. Ads cannot afford to be long-winded, because the space they occupy costs money and the audiences they are trying to reach are unlikely to care much about trying hard to get the point.

Working with clients

It is a sad fact that some of the best marketing ideas end up on the advertising equivalent of the cutting room floor. Most businesses (including very successful ones) tend to be highly conservative. Afraid of the consequences of getting it wrong, they tend to be reluctant to do anything that might rock the boat; and that usually includes embarking on outrageous advertising campaigns. As a result, most advertising tends to be a compromise between the initial creative idea and the rather more cautious views of the marketing bosses who foot the bill. This means two things for copywriters:

◆ first, you need to provide a strongly thought out rationale for why your ad campaign will work

◆ second, you need to be prepared to ditch, revise and re-work your ideas.

This process of testing and re-working ideas can, however, work to the benefit of the campaign. As mentioned above, pure creativity is not the only ingredient in successful advertising. Ads also need to bring out the right emotional response in their audiences or else they will simply be annoying. (And who has not been turned off a brand because of its 'stupid ads'?) They also (as described in Chapter 8) need to employ the right tone for both the audience and the advertiser. The compromises arrived at in the development of an ad often involve the testing of dozens of different ideas. Some of these will be weeded out by the creative team, some by the client and others by research panels.

4. Benefits and USPs

Remember *talk benefits, not features*? This is of paramount importance in advertising, because your audience simply is not going to wait around while you talk about how many flashing lights your client's latest gizmo has got. So the first thing you need to do is to work out what the key benefits of your client's product or service are for the audience it is aimed at. Then pick the one that sets your client apart from its competitors. This is your unique selling point, or USP. It is possible the USP will already have been identified by your client and may form part of your brief. It is furthermore likely that the USP will have a lot in common with your client's brand; in fact, it might be what defines your client's brand. If you think about major brands, it is usually easy to spot the USPs that they have developed over years of advertising. And remember that a product or service may have different USPs for different target audiences. Notice also that the USP is not a feature, although it may be related to features in the product or service. To find the USP, ask: 'Why should I want one of these products/services?' Then turn your answer into an emotion or a feeling. Getting this feeling across is the key to your message.

5. Maximum Impact, Minimum Copy

Your next job is to write out the message you are trying to get across, longhand. Unless you are working on a project that specifically demands a lot of copy, such as an advertorial (an advert written in the style of a press feature or news item), then you will need to cut the message down. Then cut it down again. It is fair to say that advertising copywriters are often recognised and rewarded on an inverse scale to most other copywriters: the less you write, the more you are worth. This is because you have only a split second to hit your audience with a message, so it has to be short, and it has to be good. If you are a really good copywriter, you might be able to do away with words altogether and come up with ads that get a clear idea across without even having to be read. (Apple's 1984 commercial had no scripted narrative; its idea was clear from images alone.)

Alternatively, try to distil your idea down to a single word. For maximum impact, the word might have double meaning in association with a particular image. Or it might be a derivation of another word. Study ads and work out which ones create the most impact, and why. Think of copy lines that have stood the test of time. Then try to follow similar rules in your own copywriting.

> **Here is an example. The 'They're grrreat' line for Kellogg's Frosties. It is clever, because it ties in neatly with the brand's mascot; plus it sells the product in a straightforward way. All in two words. Can you beat that?**

What works

For your main copy, refer back to Chapter 8. Write in plain, simple, straightforward English. Use short words and sentences. Avoid puns, clichés, technical terms, abbreviations.

6. Thinking In Words and Pictures

One of the most important skills in advertising copywriting is to be able to visualise your message in pictures as well as words. The brain picks up on images much more quickly than it does on the written word, so if you want to capture someone's attention it is easier to do it with a photograph or diagram than with a sentence.

In most advertising, you will notice that images are used to immediately set the scene for the copy, which effectively acts in the same way as the punch-line in a joke.

So you could, for example, try to visualise a situation where your message, the single line of copy containing your USP, will act as a pay-off.

It is also possible to use text itself as imagery. The way copy is presented, in terms of typefaces, colours and so on, can be important in helping get a message across. It can even be the substance of the message. As an example, consider the following ad for Sudafed, a decongestant, created for Pfizer Consumer Healthcare by Karl Sanderson and Dan Heady of the advertising agency Bates UK. The ad ran in Britain in 2001 on Trivision posters, which are outdoor units with slatted faces that allow up to three different copy messages to appear one after the other:

(Copyright 2001 Pfizer Consumer Healthcare)

> **Because images play such an important part in advertising, the industry norm is for a copywriter to pair up with an art director and form a team. If you are doing a significant amount of advertising work, finding an art director is practically essential; the additional creative input they can provide is invaluable.**

7. Getting a Response

The aim of advertising is to change perceptions, but many campaigns are aimed at stimulating sales, too, so it is usual to include some point of contact where a customer can find out more. This can range from a subtly-placed website address to a booking number writ large over posters and TV spots (or even aeroplanes, in the case of the budget airline easyJet).

Ads which carry a very obvious, sales-based call to action fall into a category called direct response advertising, because their intention is to stimulate an immediate purchase.

This area started off simply with telephone numbers being included in TV ads. But it has grown massively with the development of electronic communications channels such as the internet and digital television, where, because they are linked to an advertiser's website, commercials tend to be of the direct response variety by definition.

> **When taking a brief for an ad or for a campaign, check to see whether a response mechanism needs to be included and, if so, what kind.**

8. Writing For Different Media

Unlike most other forms of copywriting, where the medium for your text is fixed (on screen for the web, printed paper for direct mail and so on), advertising covers a wide range of media, each requiring different styles and obeying different rules. Writing banner ads for internet sites, for example, is a very different matter from scripting TV commercials, although in both cases you still need to abide by the basic rules of good copywriting described in Chapter 8.

Going into detail about how to approach each type of medium is beyond the scope of this book. Scriptwriting, for example, is a major field in its own right. If you are going to be doing a lot of work in this area then I would suggest you buy a specialist book or take a course on the subject. However, here are some basic pointers to bear in mind regarding the main media used in advertising, to help you with any occasional briefs that might come your way.

The types of media below are listed in rough order of importance in terms of their share of the market. (July 2007 figures from the Advertising Association showed press ad spend accounted for 43.7 per cent of total UK advertising expenditure. Figures for other media were: TV, 24.1 per cent; direct mail, 12.2 per cent; internet, 10.6 per cent; outdoor, 5.7 per cent; radio, 2.8 per cent; and cinema, 1 per cent.)

Note I have left direct mail and promotional material out of this chapter as they are covered in more detail later in this book.

> **Bear in mind that the range of media used in advertising is increasing day by day. When approaching any brief, don't just think about what your message should be, but also what medium it will work best on. Then start working on your copy.**

Print

This is by far the most frequently used medium, with formats ranging from small ads in the classified sections of newspapers to full-page display ads in glossy magazines.

Considerations for display ads are:

◆ Size and shape: will your ad work as well landscape as it does portrait?

◆ Colour or black and white: mainly a consideration for the art director or designer you are working with (if you are working in a team), but bear in mind that your copy may have to work harder if you are not able to use a very strong image.

◆ Tone and style of the publications: it goes without saying that your copy will have to fit with the kind of magazines or newspapers it is going into if it is to have the best impact with the publications' target audiences.

Television

Writing for television is the ultimate goal of any serious advertising copywriter (and, indeed, many other writers, serious or otherwise). It also demands very special skills, since your script is not only a sales tool but also a creative guide to the director who will turn your words into images and sounds.

Some considerations are:

◆ Make sure your work is in a format that a director can work with easily. Scripts need to be set in a single column down the left-hand side of the page, with dialogue indented and each actor indicated clearly in capital letters centred over their lines. As a guide, take a look at some of the scripts on specialist websites such as Simply Scripts (www.simplyscripts.com). You may also want to buy script formatting software such as Scriptware (www.scriptware.com).

◆ An art director is almost indispensable as you will need to story-board your script prior to production.

◆ Use the action – rather than the actors – to tell your tale. (For more on this, the art of 'exposition', read Robert McKee's book on cinema scriptwriting, *Story*.)

Radio

Radio is not an easy medium to write for, since your words cannot get help from visual props and you have very little time to develop an elaborate message.

Bear in mind the following:

◆ Timing is crucial. Try to pack as much impact and information as you can into each ad.

◆ It is also important that your messages are short and clear. Remember that your copy could be delivered in any number of ways and listened to in any number of environments.

◆ Think about using sound effects to bring the settings of your ads to life. If the commercial is supposed to be set in an office, for example, include office noise in the background.

◆ Jingles can be used to help deliver a consistent brand message over a number of ads or even campaigns. If your ad includes a jingle, make sure you practise it aloud to get it right – a copy line on paper will not always sound as good when it is spoken.

Outdoor

'Outdoor' basically means posters, which are broken down into size categories depending on how many sheets of paper make them up, from six sheets to 96 sheets covering 400 square feet (the 48-sheet billboard format, covering 200 square feet, is the one commonly seen on roadsides). Recent years have seen an explosion in formats, including giant posters (usually occupying special sites such as the sides of buildings) and those with Trivision (the format used by Pfizer Consumer Healthcare in the Sudafed ad example earlier on). A related type of medium is 'ambient', which refers to advertising in the environment (but not necessarily on posters) – for example, ads on the back of bus tickets. When approaching this kind of work, bear in mind:

◆ The size and location limitations of the medium you are considering, plus how it is likely to be seen by an audience. You can pack a lot of copy into a poster on a train platform, for example, because people are likely to be standing in front of it for some time. If you are writing copy for a roadside billboard, however, your message needs to stand out in the two or three seconds it may take a motorist to drive by.

◆ Whether you can use the context of the poster to drive home your message. An ad such as 'You wait ages for an X and then three come along at once' might be a bit hackneyed on the side of a bus but elsewhere you may be able to improve the effectiveness of your advertising by relating the message to its environment.

◆ Whether it is possible to use the medium itself to boost the effectiveness of your copy. I once worked on a campaign (with the PR agency Band & Brown Communications) where we built a client's free-phone number in giant numerals on a hillside at the side of a motorway in the West Country, England; what made the campaign effective was not so much that it was seen by motorists but that it made the news, along with an explanation of the aims of the campaign.

Online

The classic format for online advertising is the banner ad, that ubiquitous commercial strip which has become a constant in most website designs. Nowadays there are many other formats including 'towers' (vertical banner ads), 'buttons' (square boxes) and ultra-annoying pop-ups, which leap onto your screen and slow your computer down whenever you try to access a new site.

Points to bear in mind when producing online ad copy include:

◆ Stick to really simple messages. Online ads are small and limitations on screen definition mean you have to use relatively large type (although some fonts, such as Verdana, have been specially designed to be legible on-screen even at tiny point sizes).

◆ Think in frames, but do not overdo it. Animated gifs, the standard used
for most banner ads, allow you to build up a message in any number of
frames. If you go overboard, however, you run the risk of losing or
boring your audience before you get your message across, so stick to
between around three and six frames per ad unless you need more for
special animation effects.

◆ Beware of the size of the file you are creating. Most media owners
restrict the file size of banner ads to 12 kilobytes; you can, however, get
around this problem by using a Flash animation for your ad. If in doubt,
talk to a graphic designer.

◆ Online media are designed to be interactive, so make sure your ads are,
too. At the very least they should be designed to encourage the viewer to
click on them, so they will be taken to the advertiser's web site. For more
on what other types of interactivity can be built into your ads, talk to a
web design agency – you will probably be working with one on this kind
of project anyway.

See Chapter 13 for more about writing online.

11

Writing for Direct Mail

1. The Basics

Compared with the cost of taking out an advertisement, the expense involved in sending someone a letter is minimal. This is probably one reason why so much promotional material is sent directly to would-be customers in the post, a medium known generically in the trade as 'direct mail' and familiar to most recipients (perhaps more accurately) as 'junk mail'. The amount of direct mail that gets sent out in the UK is huge. Figures are available from organisations such as the Direct Marketing Association, but you can probably get a good idea just by sifting through your own post. Ironically, most of it is a complete waste of time for both the sender and the recipient. Response rates of around more than two per cent are considered exceptional. So why do people bother?

The reason is that direct mail (commonly abbreviated to DM) is still cheap enough to yield a decent return even with such high levels of waste. In the same way that fish lay large numbers of eggs in the hope that a few of their offspring will reach adulthood, direct marketers hope to hit their targets by getting a few-per-cent return on mail-shots of several thousands of items. There is a downside, however, which is that if this few per cent does not materialise then the whole exercise can be a costly waste of money. Not only that, but poorly-targeted and shoddily-produced material can, like bad advertising, have the opposite effect to what is desired and end up turning off potential customers. As a copywriter, it is your job to ensure the creative treatment used in a direct mail piece helps to boost this magical few per cent.

2. Selling By Mail

Consider the medium you are working with and how it is used by the audience you are trying to reach. Letters are a personal form of communication – hence the surge in post at special times such as, say, Christmas or Easter. Anything which is less than personal is likely to be ignored or, even worse, seen as an intrusive annoyance.

Because direct mail involves large mailing lists (typically counted in the hundreds of thousands), it can hardly be described as personal. Couple this with the fact that DM usually contains a fairly overt sales message and it is clear why so many of its recipients are infuriated by it.

If you do not want to be seen to be clogging up letterboxes with information about products or services your audience has no interest in, your copy needs to get personal and grab people's attention.

3. The Importance of Targeting

Personalisation is not merely about using a name taken from a mailing list. Although it helps if a letter is accurately addressed to a person rather than just 'the occupier' or 'the general manager', be aware that while a personalised address might fool the recipient into opening the envelope, it is unlikely to make a sale unless the message inside is relevant. In fact, some people are affronted by the fact that an organisation that so clearly knows nothing about them has presumed to adopt such a cloyingly chummy tone.

What is more, it is common for companies to use the wrong name in the first place. According to Experian Intact, an online data cleansing service, each year more than £18 million is wasted trying to reach the 1.5 million people in the UK who move home, generating 500,000 postcode changes, and the approximately 700,000 people who die. It is also illegal (under the Data Protection Act) to contact people who do not want to be mailed marketing material, so, in the UK, mailing lists have to be 'cleared' against the 240,000 per year who register their names and addresses on the Mailing Preference Service database.

Different laws cover business-to-business mailing lists, but these tend to be even more inaccurate than the consumer ones, because so many people change their jobs, titles and locations each year.

The copywriter is seldom involved in the selection of a mailing list, but she or he will be expected to write copy which mirrors the lifestyle of the people on that list.

The list will contain the names of people who meet certain criteria. They may be house owners who live in a specific location, such as London, or they may own a specific brand of car, or read a particular magazine. Although your words may be going out to several thousand strangers, you have to find a way of making them feel that you are writing to each one personally.

Look at the criteria used to specify the list and try to work out what all these people have in common. Try to get into their heads. Find out what makes them tick. Think of the care and time you would take in writing to a friend and apply the same principles to your copy. Be courteous and honest and get straight to the point, because the recipient's time is every bit as precious to him or her as yours is to you.

4. Being Creative

Your copy will have to be more than merely polite if you are to make an impact. Think how much junk lands on your doormat every day and you will see just how much 'background noise' you must cut through to create an impression. You need to do something special to grab the recipient's attention the minute they open that letter. One of the great joys (or challenges) of DM copywriting is that it demands a high level of creativity within a relatively confined format. *You must try to fit your imagination into an envelope.* To do this, go back to the benefits and USPs discussed in the last chapter. Think about what makes your client's product or service stand out. Then try to build a message around it that will appeal to your reader's emotions. And do not forget to stick to the principles of good copywriting discussed in Chapter 8.

Do not be limited to the traditional printed paper format of your mailer. Apart from perishables, poisonous substances and very delicate items, there are plenty of things you can post. Imagine you have been briefed to write a mail piece for a car dealer. You could send prospects a letter extolling the virtues of the latest models in the showroom, or you could send a car key and the message, 'Yours for the duration of a test drive' printed on the fob. Instead of a piece of marketing collateral, you are giving someone the real key to a real car. Which is more likely to generate an emotional response?

Covering letters

It has been proved time and again, over decades, in tens of thousands of test mailings, that no matter what else you send to people, if you enclose an accompanying letter it will boost response. Letters are seen as a one-to-one form of communication and even a standard letter mailed to thousands of customers can be a powerful business tool if it is properly crafted.

DM letter copy used to be personalised in a relatively crude way, by changing the product make or altering references to family members. Nowadays, however, many versions of each paragraph, or 'module', are written up so that they can be combined to make up hundreds of different letters – each relevant to a different type of lifestyle and life-stage. This allows the marketer to put together completely different sales propositions for different groups of people within a single database. The writing is only part of the story; the databases themselves are extremely sophisticated and new digital printing techniques have made it possible to produce high-quality letters to even small groups of people, at relatively low cost.

A tried and tested medium

Almost every aspect of writing for direct mail has been carefully tried, tested and tested again, until it has become a honed craft. Testing is a vital part of each new campaign, too. Typically, a client has to mail hundreds of thousands of packs to even hope to cover their costs. Otherwise, they will have to spend more on copywriter, designer, printer, stationer, mailing house, marketing department and so on than they could ever cover from the number of sales generated (unless they are selling Rolls Royces or aeroplanes). A mass-mailing is more likely to be counted in the millions than thousands or tens of thousands. To make sure it is not an expensive failure, a mailer will test a mail shot on a run of, say, 5,000 packs. Each pack can have anything up to 30 different components. Usually, five or six of these are tested, including, for example, the envelope, the response mechanism and three or four different messages.

5. Clinching the Deal

Obviously, the whole point about DM is that you are trying to sell something. But how do you go about it without being too obvious?

The best option is to switch the emphasis from selling to 'giving'. This offer can take many forms: money-off vouchers, a free consultation, preferred rates, a no-obligation trial or access to privileged information, for example. Suddenly, your mailer stops being junk mail and becomes a valuable piece of communication. Even if your prospect does not need the thing you are offering, he or she is more likely to feel pleased that you brought it to their attention.

Offering something to the customer helps to justify your reason for mailing. The subliminal message is: 'Here's something we thought you ought to know about'. This apparent altruism may go some way to overcoming any objections the customer might have to being targeted in the first place, or to receiving a letter which is poorly targeted. It also gives you an excuse to continue sending mail to the same prospect and thus, ideally, build up some kind of commercial relationship with him or her.

If you are just writing copy for a mailer it is unlikely you will be able to decide whether or how you can spend large amounts of your client's money on an incentive. However, it is worth asking whether your client is prepared to give something away in order to get a foot in the customer's door.

Another option is to find a way of treating the entire mailing as an offer or benefit. For example: 'Be one of the first in the country to try this new product and save money with our cost-effective service,' or 'We can guarantee product/service X will help to increase your profits'.

Once you have turned your sales pitch into an offer, you need to make sure your target can respond to it. A direct mail piece should always include a response mechanism – an invitation to buy or to contact your client. The more response routes you can offer, the more you will help to increase response. Options might include phone, email, fax or post. Pre-paid envelopes and free-phone numbers also stimulate extra replies.

6. Some Golden Rules for DM Copywriters

◆ Make it really easy for customers to get in touch and make sure they see the telephone number, email address or whatever by displaying them in bigger type and in a prominent position within the layout.

◆ When given the choice, respondents will usually prefer to use the telephone – but some, such as older consumers, prefer coupons.

◆ If you ask questions, frame them so they can be answered with a 'yes', 'no' or 'don't know' response, so respondents merely have to tick a box.

◆ Any device which makes it easier and faster to complete a form or coupon will also increase the response.

◆ Always put coupons on the outside edge of a letter, preferably with perforations, so they can be detached easily.

◆ Never ask too many questions because it is easy to put people off before they even start.

◆ Always ask the most important questions first, just in case the recipient runs out of steam halfway through the coupon or questionnaire.

◆ Customers can be extremely lazy or inattentive, so make it *really easy* for them to understand what you are offering and how they can take advantage of it.

◆ Clients can sometimes miss a trick or two, as well. When you take a brief, make sure you understand exactly how they expect to deliver the mailer, handle responses, deal with problems and so on. For example, do they want to include a response coupon within the copy? And, if so, where?

◆ Has the client remembered to tell you about any small print that needs to be included? Is there any information that is legally required? Has the client fulfilled their obligations under the Data Protection Act by giving customers the opportunity to opt out of being contacted by the company, or other companies, in the future? Offers and competitions usually have conditions that you will need to include in your word count. Mailers for certain types of professional services, such as financial investments, need to carry a legend relating to their eligibility to offer advice, and so on.

◆ If you can, talk to the fulfilment company that will be on the receiving end of any replies. A large part of the value of DM comes from 'data capture' – gathering information from respondents – and the way you word questions can make a big difference to how easy and costly this is.

7. Consumer and Business-To-Business Audiences

An important distinction in direct mail and indeed in many other areas of copywriting is whether your messages are aimed at the general public (or sections of it) or businesses. Nowadays these two markets are often known by the abbreviations they were given during the dotcom boom – 'b2c' for 'business-to-consumer' and 'b2b' for 'business-to-business'. Some of the differences between these two types of work are:

◆ In consumer marketing, the average number of prospects targeted tends to be larger.

◆ Targeting in b2b tends to be by industry sector and job title.

◆ In both areas the key is to get the attention of the purchase decision-maker, but in b2b this can be more difficult because mail is often intercepted by 'gatekeepers' – secretaries, private assistants and so on.

◆ Because people move jobs and companies so often, it is almost impossible to keep business-to-business lists up to date and accurate.

8. Email Marketing

Recent years have seen a massive surge in the popularity of email as a medium to supplement or replace traditional mail in DM, to the point where few b2b campaigns (and an increasing number of b2c campaigns) are complete without an email component. There is a good number of reasons for this popularity, such as:

◆ Email delivery is around three or four orders of magnitude cheaper than post, plus it is virtually instantaneous.

◆ With email you can tell automatically when a message is opened or an address is defunct.

◆ It is much easier for customers to respond to email, either via a reply-to address or a link to a website.

◆ Emails can also easily be sent to other personal electronic devices, such as personal digital assistants or mobile phones.

Given these (and other) benefits, it is a shame that a number of less-than-scrupulous email marketers have spoilt the pitch for the rest of the industry by flooding inboxes around the world with unsolicited commercial email or 'spam'. (The common name is thought to have been derived from a Monty Python sketch in which Spam, a meat product, was offered with everything on sale in a café.)

If you use a common email platform such as Microsoft Hotmail, you can end up getting several hundred spam emails a week. Even extreme low-grade spam (of which there is an awful lot) is often made to appear legitimate by the inclusion of an 'unsubscribe' opt-out link that promises to remove the user from the mailing list their address was found on.

Selecting this option is worse than doing nothing, however; it will either lead to a dead-end link or, more likely, alert the list user to the fact that your email is alive, so your address can be re-sold to other spammers.

Given that most people (and companies) pay for their email and internet connections and are wasting both money and time whenever they have to deal with spam, it is not surprising that unsolicited email is a major bane for both targets and the internet and DM industries in general. Legitimate email marketers usually work with lists where users have specifically stated they want to receive information; these are either built up in-house from an existing customer-base or shared between commercial partners with the express consent of the user.

Spam, though, is often difficult to tell from bona-fide opt-in communications (called 'permission-based marketing' in the industry), which means most email users soon get wary of anything that looks like a commercial message and filter it out.

There are other drawbacks to the medium that you need to be aware of, too:

◆ Even without spam, the number of email messages being sent around the world is growing to the point where a typical user is likely to get overwhelmed. It is said that a typical business user spends over two hours a day just dealing with email.

◆ Although most email platforms allow you to receive messages (called HTML emails) with formatting, images and other design elements, you cannot guarantee all your targets will see these as intended. So, design-wise, email marketing offers two options: either send out HTML emails and bear in mind that a proportion of your prospects may end up getting a messy mix of text and computer code, or stick to plain text with no formatting whatsoever.

◆ Unlike postal addresses, not everyone you may want to reach has got email and certain sectors of the population are not likely to have it for some time (although, from a marketing perspective, it may be possible to reach some of these with mobile text messaging instead).

Tips for direct email copywriting

Bearing in mind the above, you should:

◆ Write text that will have impact on its own, without formatting, unless you are reasonably certain that your targets can receive HTML email.

◆ Avoid anything in the subject line that may make the email look like spam. This includes multiple exclamation marks (or, indeed, any exclamation marks), nonspecific subjects ('hey'; 'I thought you might be interested in this'; and so on), all-caps and truncated or corrupted headings ('HEY!!!!! I THOUGHT YOU MIGHT BExguqua').

Things that will help make your emails more effective include:

◆ Coming from a reputable source (a category which hopefully includes your clients).

◆ Having a subject line that offers a clear and obvious reason for being read ('Improve your customer retention by 10%' rather than 'News from Company X', for example).

◆ Talking benefits right up front.

◆ Using a tone that is informal, but not necessarily chummy. Remember that emails are more personal than letters.

◆ Breaking up your copy into small chunks, to make it easier to read. Ideally, you should have no more than three lines together on screen and put a paragraph space in between every sentence. Break your paragraphs with one-line spaces.

◆ Using keyboard symbols, where necessary, to help with formatting. For example, if you need to put a line between paragraphs, use a series of dashes (———) or equals signs (= = = =).

Email newsletters

Email newsletters, often linked to a website, are a common and inexpensive form of corporate communication whose use ranges from traditional publishing through customer relationship management to internal communications.

The basic guidelines of email writing outlined above apply just as well to electronic newsletters, although there is more scope for bending the rules because you are usually talking to an audience that has specifically requested a regular communication from your client.

It will help to have some technical knowledge of web-based communications as, for example, being able to send HTML emails can make a big difference to the appearance and readability of your publication.

Electronic newsletters also have much in common with traditional publications (see Chapter 14), such as the need to create and adhere to a style guide.

If you are involved in this line of work, whether as an editor, producer or just an occasional contributor, it would be worthwhile subscribing to a few email newsletters yourself to get a feel for the medium.

> **There are many to choose from; some of my personal favourites are The Grok (www.grokdotcom.com), The Motley Fool (www.fool.co.uk) and The Register (www.theregister.co.uk).**

12

Writing for Internal Communications

1. What Is Internal Communications?

These days, almost any organisation with more than a couple of hundred employees is likely to have some form of regular, written staff communication, providing a rich source of potential work for copywriters. The traditional format for employee (or 'internal') communications has always been the magazine or newsletter. These can vary in quality from a simple photocopied sheet of A4 (which still abounds at departmental level) to, in large companies, professionally-written and designed newspapers with circulations to rival those of their commercial equivalents. Increasingly, however, the newsletter is being replaced or supplemented by other media, such as intranets (websites used within companies), email newsletters and even business television. In addition, internal communications work often involves occasional one-off projects, such as the production of posters or flyers, to raise awareness of specific developments such as office moves or reorganisations.

The aim of most programmes is to keep staff (and/or *be seen* to keep staff) informed of developments in the business, working on the principle that informed employees will be happier and therefore more productive employees.

Some things you need to know about internal communications

♦ Employees – the people being targeted by internal communications – are usually rightly mistrustful of what they read and tend to take it with a pinch of salt. They believe what they hear on the grapevine.

♦ People in middle management love internal communications because it gives them a platform to showcase what they do to the rest of their business. They will be more than keen to help and can end up making unreasonable demands in their efforts to promote themselves and their teams ('Why can't you include the names of everyone in the department?' is one question I have heard more than once in relation to a minor story in an internal communications publication).

♦ Senior management – the people who approve funding for internal communications – often see it as a vaguely necessary but inconveniently costly by-product of hiring staff. They are all the more likely to be irked by the fact that it is rarely possible to quantify any tangible benefit from the exercise.

2. Processes Involved in Internal Communications Programmes

Internal communications programmes can be split into two categories; those that mainly rely on an in-house resource (either a single editor or a full editorial team) and those where the bulk of the writing and design is farmed out, usually to specialist agencies. In the latter case, the business will usually appoint an internal 'editor' who has an overseeing role, perhaps approving story leads and copy, but does not directly produce content. Both types of programme call for freelance copywriting support from time to time, either to cover for editorial or agency staff shortages, or sometimes to provide more long-term help with content. You may even be asked to design, implement and run an entire programme yourself.

Regardless of which of the above categories they fall into, and whether they involve a magazine, an intranet site, or other media (or, indeed, a mix of media), most internal communications programmes have a number of features in common:

◆ They tend to be initiated and led by marketing departments rather than human resources or finance. This may be because internal communications is usually seen as an in-house extension of a business's external public relations efforts.

◆ Depending on the seniority of the editor, it is not unusual for copy (or page proofs) to require approval from one or several senior executives in the business before it can be published.

◆ There may also be a network or panel of other people in the client organisation, perhaps from different departments around the business, who are responsible for feeding story leads into and gathering feedback for the programme.

Typically, internal communications programmes all follow a similar production process, too, regardless of how frequently material is published:

◆ Story leads are put forward and agreed upon at the beginning of the production cycle, often in a face-to-face meeting. This may also include a review of activity just completed (usually the last edition of the magazine/newsletter).

◆ Stories are then researched, usually by interviewing agreed contacts in the business, and written up.

◆ Once each story is written, it then goes back to the contact for checking and approval. The copywriter is usually in charge of this process.

◆ At the same time, requirements for any further items associated with the story (such as photographs) are followed up. This task, again, quite often falls to the writer.

◆ The approved story will then often go through one or two more clearance stages, for example via an in-house editor and a senior member of management, before it can be published.

3. Striking The Right Tone

Every internal communications programme has to satisfy two opposing requirements. On the one hand, it has to act as a channel for messages from the management that is funding it. On the other, if it is to be accepted by the employee audience it is aimed at, it cannot appear to be a corporate mouthpiece. Most good internal communications programmes get round this dilemma by at least appearing to retain some semblance of objectivity.

They do this by facing up to tough issues like redundancies or pay cuts and talking about them honestly, albeit with a likely bias towards the more positive aspects of the news. They may also feature 'softer' topics like fundraising events or personal hobbies, both to make the communication more varied and readable and to show 'it ain't all work'.

Do these measures have any bearing on employee attitudes and behaviour? I think they do, but only insofar as the employee communications programme is usually a reflection of the underlying culture of a business.

I have certainly had first-hand experience of employee magazines with surprisingly loyal and enthusiastic followings, but it is fair to say that these have tended to belong to businesses with relatively honest, transparent employee policies. Under these circumstances, I believe most employees recognise the corporate nature of internal communications, but take a pragmatic view that any news from the business they work in is better than no news, and so are happy to go along with what they are being told. Provided, of course, it is not too much at odds with the information they get from other sources, like the grapevine.

Even assuming you are working with a business that recognises the value of open and honest communications it is still essential to recognise that the purpose of internal communications is to impart corporate messages to a mainly sceptical audience.

When writing for internal communications, you need to become adept at judging your client's corporate culture so that you can 'sell' management messages in a tone and style of language which employees will buy into. It should come as no surprise to know that the style that tends to work best is one that is simple and straightforward – exactly the opposite of most management communications.

4. Dealing With Approvals

While researching copy for internal communications is usually fairly straightforward, often involving no more than a call to someone in a particular department, the approval process that follows can be extremely trying.

Here again, two opposing forces can come into play. To begin with, as a competent and conscientious copywriter, you will produce a draft that tells the story in the simplest, most interesting way possible, following the rules of good copywriting outlined in Chapter 8. But your contacts within the organisation, whether they are the people you speak to in researching the story or those that have the final veto, may well feel that they want the story told in a different way, and introduce all sorts of changes when they are asked to clear the copy.

If these changes are to do with factual accuracy then there should be no reason to challenge them, unless they contradict something you have already double-checked yourself. Similarly, cosmetic changes to direct quotes (made by the people being quoted) should not present a problem. But as often as not you might be confronted with partial or complete re-writes which impair the readability of the story, contravene in-house rules on style or even introduce grammatically incorrect language. (The use of the plural instead of the singular when referring to organisations or departments, as in 'Company X are,' is a common offence.)

How you choose to deal with these changes, or indeed whether you choose to ignore them, will vary depending on the sensitivities of each client and the strength of your working relationship with them. Generally, though, I would recommend the following when handling corrections:

◆ Admit factual corrections and changes to direct quotes.

◆ Challenge corrections that are nonsensical, grammatically incorrect or contravene house style.

◆ If a lot of the revised copy needs to be challenged, then re-draft it correctly using as much of the revised copy as possible and staying true to the meaning of the revisions elsewhere.

◆ If you have made substantial changes to the approved version, send it back for a second approval, along with an explanation of why you have made your changes.

These measures will usually be sufficient to resolve any clashes between you and your client's choice of language use. In some cases, though, the client may insist on sticking with their version. As always in these situations, what you do next will largely be dictated by your relationship with your client. If you cannot appeal to a higher authority, the easiest solution can sometimes be to capitulate and live to write another day.

5. Creating and Maintaining a Style Guide

Your discussions over the correct use of words and language in copy can be greatly helped if you have a style guide to refer to. Style guides are intended to provide guidance on general language use and advice on specific areas such as industry-related jargon or acronyms. They are important not just in internal communications, but also in most other areas of publishing, from web content to magazine and newspaper writing.

Most large, established companies already have some form of in-house style guide, particularly if they publish a fair amount of material. However, there may be occasions where you are required to develop one yourself; or where the existing style guide is inadequate (for example, because it is mainly concerned with the way the corporate logo should be portrayed) and you have to extend or adapt it. Putting together a comprehensive style guide can take days or even weeks, but is worth it in terms of resolving issues over the correct use of terms in corporate materials.

The aim of a style guide is to ensure consistency in written materials, so when compiling a guide you need to consider all areas of writing that may be open to interpretation. Examples of things to cover include:

- **General language issues**: does the company use UK or US spelling? Is the writing style to be formal and sophisticated or informal and chatty?

- **Names and titles**: are people referred to by their first names or last names? Are titles capped up or lower case? How is the business referred to?

- **Locations**: how does the business refer to its subsidiaries, trading regions and so on?

- **Numbers**: when are numbers spelt out? When are they written in numerals? How do you write monetary amounts, millions and so on?

- **Abbreviations**: do you write 'per cent' or '%'? Which corporate or industry abbreviations are well known enough to be used routinely?

- **Brand names**: how are they spelt and written?

- **Slogans and special notices**: are there any texts (often called 'strap-lines') that have to be associated with brand names or with particular types of copy?

- **Special words**: are there any words or phrases that have special use or are to be avoided?

If you are writing a style guide from scratch, it may help to use an existing newspaper guide for reference; you can buy copies of the style guides used by major papers like the Financial Times *or* The Times. *It is also useful to hang on to copies of style guides that you may come across in your work for clients.*

Chapter 8 in this book contains pointers on a number of areas that you will probably want to include.

Once you have drafted a guide, you will probably need to get your client to approve it. This can be a useful process, helping your client understand the importance of having a professional copywriter on board but also giving you valuable insights into the way that the business you are working with thinks about and refers to itself.

> Even after your style guide has been approved, it will probably need to be revised at regular intervals as new terms are added and guidance on brand- or industry-related areas changes. Make sure that the guide is widely available, too, so that it gets used and adopted by as many people as possible.

6. Human Interest and Business Stories

Most internal communications programmes follow a philosophy that runs along the lines of: 'what is important is the news about the business but what is going to help staff read it is news about people'. Human-interest stories – those concerning the exploits of individuals rather than businesses – not only tend to be lighter (and thus easier to read and digest), but also help engender team spirit. Plus they can create a sense that the business is an organisation that cares for its people and is willing to devote space to them in its corporate communications.

As a result, it is fairly usual for internal communications programmes to try to strike a balance between business and human-interest stories, often devoting several news items and sometimes even a special page to sporting and social events.

Employee magazines or papers may even have a 'coffee time' page with quizzes, crosswords, cartoons, gardening columns and so on.

Human-interest stories need to be treated quite differently from business items. The tone is usually much lighter and may even be tongue-in-cheek. Use of first names is the norm. But it is just as important to seek approval of the subject matter; employees are just as likely to get upset about being misquoted about their favourite hobby as they are for an error in a story regarding a new management initiative.

Maximising the interest in human interest

You would never believe some of the things people do when they get out of the office. I have written stories about staff doing everything from collecting airline sick bags to taking part in horse-and-trap races.

Sadly, such exploits tend to be the exception rather than the norm. Most human interest stories revolve around the kinds of things many people do on a regular basis: playing sports at amateur level, raising cash for charity, playing in a band and so on. When covering these, it is of course possible to write up a straight account of the news. But while a five-a-side football game between two different offices, for example, may have been great fun for the people involved, it is hardly going to leap off the page in terms of a story.

To make the most of these stories you often have to go beyond the event itself in search of something truly amusing or memorable. Dig deep for details when you speak to your source. In this five-a-side contest, did the novice team trounce the expert players? Was there anything special about the winning goal-scorer? Was this the culmination of a trend? Was there any special significance in the date, the location, the players or whatever? You may find, for example, that the coach carrying one team nearly had an accident and only the quick intervention of a player saved the team from disaster – a much more powerful story than your original lead.

Business stories

The principle of trying to raise interest also applies to business stories – and perhaps with greater justification. Management is often keen to lay out in detail plans for improved productivity, rationalisation, reorganisation and so on. For employees, such issues usually boil down to a simple question: 'What does it mean for me?' (Which, in some cases, can be roughly restated as: 'Will I keep my job?') The management response to this is usually of the form: 'We are doing this to improve the business and if the business does well then we all do well'. (There may also be a few 'buts' involved.) However, it is important, both for the credibility of the internal communications programme and for the readability of the story, that the 'what does it mean for me?' question is addressed up front.

Also, since business stories may sometimes convey news that is of critical importance to the livelihood of workers, it is vital that they are written in a formal, sensitive way. It is also vital that they are written. Business leaders often like to think they can keep the lid on bad news, such as redundancies, for as long as possible. In fact, such news leaks out almost the minute it is formulated (if it has not been predicted already) and spreads out through the organisation via the grapevine. A good internal communications programme will recognise this and put out an official (if often necessarily brief) statement at the earliest possible opportunity. Employees appreciate being told, even if what they are being told is only that there will be more news to follow.

7. Managing Internal Communications Programmes

If you are called upon to manage a staff communications programme rather than simply contribute to it, then you will need to become familiar with a number of production processes as well as the actual generation of copy. Points you will need to monitor include:

- **Schedules**: what needs to be done by when? If you are devising your own schedule, remember to give yourself plenty of time for each step in the process, in case you miss something out or something goes wrong. It is also easier to increase the frequency of communications than to decrease them.

- **Costs**: apart from your own time, what is the budget allocation for photography, design, distribution and other costs such as couriers or meetings? Are the costs realistic? If you are unsure, get a few quotes for each type of activity and then add a five or ten per cent contingency figure on top.

◆ **Images**: how many do you need per issue or per month? What format do you need them in? Will you be commissioning them yourself or will they come from stock sources such as photo libraries? How many of them will be contributed free? Will there be any copyright issues? If possible, make sure that you have the budget to cover photographers' fees.

◆ **Design and production**: will you be working alongside a designer to produce pages? What is their turnaround time? How much will they charge? Who in the client organisation will approve page designs? Remember that designers tend to charge every time you make corrections to the copy on a page, so it is best to make sure all text is fully approved before you send it off to be laid out.

◆ **Print**: who will print (or post online) the pages you plan to publish? Again, what are their turnaround times and their costs? How will you get to see proofs of the printed pages? How will printed copies be distributed to employees?

◆ **Feedback and story generation**: how will you gather leads? Is there a panel of correspondents around the business that you can use? Can you set one up? How will you measure the success of the programme?

Do not underestimate the amount of work involved in managing an internal communications programme. The job of keeping tabs on all the different stages of production, from gathering leads and getting copy approval to commissioning photography and checking proofs, can easily dwarf the amount of time you spend writing.

Different media

As with other areas of copywriting, the medium you are communicating in can have a profound impact on the style and content you employ in internal communications. Here are some considerations that you need to be aware of regarding each medium:

◆ **Staff newspapers, newsletters or magazines** will often reflect the style of a commercial publication relevant to the social mix of the workforce. In one agency I worked at, *The Daily Mirror* was used as a rough template for virtually all employee newspapers; other large company publications have a similar look and feel to regional papers. However, one area in which employee publications can rarely match their commercial counterparts is in frequency. Printing on anything more than a monthly schedule is usually prohibitively expensive and, because print and design are normally farmed out, the turnaround time for production can be days if not weeks. So printed media tend to be rather poor at delivering up-to-date or time-sensitive news. They are also costly, but are preferred by many organisations (and employees) because the printed page is a familiar, easy-to-read format.

◆ **Intranets** provide a cheap, quick and easy way of providing information to employees. Normal rules of web copywriting (see next chapter) apply; text must be simple and short, which makes intranets a poor medium for conveying complex or in-depth messages. Also, there can be delivery problems if employees do not have access to computers or are too busy or lazy to check the intranet for new content. On the plus side, intranet stories can easily be linked to other archive materials and text can easily be changed after it has been posted (a boon for internal spin doctors).

◆ **Email** is increasingly used for internal communications because it is cheap and easy to use. Email newsletters can be put together and distributed in a fraction of the time it takes to assemble a printed publication, and for a fraction of the cost. It is easier to quantify the benefits of the medium, too; you can measure how many people open the email and, if it is linked to stories online, how many of those get read. For obvious reasons, though, email newsletters only really work well when all the target audience has access to a computer, so their application is limited in sectors such as manufacturing.

◆ **Business television** is still something of a rarity but is likely to increase in popularity as traditional broadcast systems are replaced by digital distribution via corporate networks. For those entrusted with producing content, the onus is not so much on copywriting as on finding material that will provide good images: interviews, location shots and so on. The medium is still relatively expensive and can suffer from distribution problems if staff cannot all get to a screen. But it remains a good medium, other than a face-to-face meeting, for issuing critical news where people really need to know exactly what is being said.

◆ **Other types of media** used in internal communications range from information-based screen savers to CD-ROMs, although none of these at present looks likely to achieve the popularity of the methods described above. There is one final type of communication, however, that should be mentioned: talking. This supersedes every other form in its effectiveness and you will rarely go wrong by recommending it as a means of improving internal communications.

13

Writing for the Internet

1. A Short History of the Internet

The origins of the internet can be traced back to the 60s, when the US Defence Advanced Research Projects Agency devised a communications network called ARPANET which could still work even if parts of the whole had been knocked out by a disaster or attack. Over the years this network developed into what we now call the internet. For decades, however, the system was difficult to use without technical knowledge, and so was adopted only by military and scientific establishments, for basic communications such as email.

In the early 90s, however, two related developments changed all that. The first was the invention of a computer code called hypertext mark-up language (HTML). This made it possible to format text, pictures, colours and patterns on a screen to create what are known as web pages (so called because they are distributed over a section of the internet called the world-wide web). The second was the introduction of programs called web browsers that could read HTML and thus allow users to view these pages.

These developments came as personal computers (PCs) plummeted in price and started to become a feature in many homes. A few companies realised there could be a market in giving consumers at home access to the internet via a telephone line and modem, even though at first the medium had little more to offer than email and other text-based services such as news groups. Top among these companies was America Online (AOL), which built its own network, linked to the internet, and used HTML web pages to make it easy for people to communicate with each other in communities of interest. (Although AOL's proprietory network probably did much to entice early users onto the internet by giving them an easy way of finding their way around, other companies, known traditionally as internet service providers or ISPs, have by and large simply provided access to whatever is out there.)

As interest in the internet increased, a growing number of individuals and companies started adding their own sites to the network (this process is not difficult provided you have access to a computer, called a server, linked to the internet at all times). By the mid-90s, not only was there quite a lot to see on the internet, but getting online was relatively easy, too. The number of ISPs had grown, web browser programs were easy to get hold of and the hardware needed (usually just a box called a modem) was getting cheaper by the week. As if by magic, a vast new medium appeared to have sprung out of nowhere. The flurry of excitement about internet-based businesses that followed, the dotcom boom and subsequent bust, touched virtually the whole of the global economy and is of course very well documented.

The next big development related to the internet was broadband, a technology which gives you a permanent connection to the world-wide web and allows you to view video clips and listen to music online. Meanwhile, there has also been great interest in adapting web-based content to other digital platforms, such as mobile phones and interactive television.

At one point it looked as though the apparently unstoppable growth of new media would create a never-ending demand for copy. While this has clearly failed to be the case, the fact that most websites need a constant supply of new material means there are still great opportunities for writers, provided they can demonstrate that they know how to write for the medium.

The bottom line for copywriters

The web has created an important market for copy by upping the demand for constantly changing content. This market is vastly different from other media, however; consider, for example, that a web page can be viewed by 500 million people within seconds of leaving your PC. These pages can remain in archives for years. They can be linked to, copied and translated over and over. While it is possible to impose rights on the content you produce, so it is available to some and not to others, in general your work will live on the web forever and be available to any and all for whatever purpose they want.

2. The Basics of Web Copy

When people first started putting text on the internet there was little or no notion of the limitations of the medium. Many of the results (some of which are still around today) were not dissimilar to those of the early days of desktop publishing in the 80s, with an enthusiasm for unusual fonts and colours sometimes making text all but unreadable.

By the mid-90s, however, as an increasing number of professional communicators turned to the internet out of personal and commercial interest, a body of wisdom began to grow regarding what would and would not work on the web. From this, a set of basic rules emerged that is now fairly well established, if not necessarily well known to those outside the web copywriting fraternity.

The starting point is the simple fact that text is harder to read on screen than it is on paper. It takes longer to read the same number of words and it can be difficult to track sentences in large blocks of text. When you scroll down a page, it becomes even more difficult to keep track of where you are. In fact, knowing where you are generally on a website is more difficult than it is with physical media; the page you were looking at two moments ago can be hard to find again once you have moved on. This 'jumpy' nature of content, made possible through hypertext links between pages, also means that you may not finish reading one piece of text before you find yourself in another.

It is all very confusing. Which is why virtually all the rules that govern good web copy are concerned with making text *easy to read, easy to assimilate and easy to move around in*. The basic rules (with variations depending on whom you consult) are:

◆ Break text up into short chunks. Very short chunks. No more than about 50 words per paragraph.

- Make each paragraph a self-contained statement.

- Make that statement worth reading. Remember that bored readers will be on another page (or site) at the click of a mouse.

- Make the overall text short, too. No more than about two screens' worth of copy. That's 300 to 400 words.

- If your text is longer than that, try breaking it into sections that can go on different web pages.

- Finally, if a piece of long text absolutely has to stay together, give each paragraph or two a heading and put links to each heading at the top of the page; the reader can jump to any section they want to. Make sure there is a return link with each heading, as well, so that readers can easily get back to the point they came from.

Getting to the point

In effect, the creation of good web copy is nothing more than another application of the 'keep it short' principle covered in Chapter 8. When writing for the web, you need to cut out all the frills and niceties of language and get straight to the point. No word should be too precious to spare from the edit.

On the web it is more important than ever to use small words instead of large ones. But because of space constraints and the need to impart information quickly, it is also more usual to use contractions ('it's' instead of 'it is', for example) in web copy.

Web readers do not want to hang around reading your copy, but they do need to be entertained by it. Unlike other types of media, the internet is full of opportunities for interaction. Your text will be competing with pictures, flashing banner ads, pop-up windows and all manner of other enticements. Even when you have got only 250 words it can be a tough job getting anyone to read till the end.

As important as it is to keep your message short, then, you need to make sure it is interesting, relevant and/or amusing. Many websites try to achieve this by adopting a personal, chatty tone with their readers. While this may well engage most audiences, I would favour doing whatever you think is right for the particular readers of the site you are writing for.

Editing for the web

One of the less surprising facts about the internet is that people tend to be more interested in revisiting websites if there is something new there for them to see. As a consequence, the principle of updating content as often as possible has become enshrined in web best practice, happily for copywriters and others who are charged with supplying that content. News sites, for example, often post up new stories on an ongoing basis, so publication happens almost as soon as a story is written.

This voracious appetite for content on the web means editors are usually keen to re-use material that has been published elsewhere. As a copywriter, therefore, it is not unusual for you to be asked to adapt your (or indeed, another person's) press feature, brochure text, case study or whatever for use online.

If the text is already short and punchy, this should not usually present a problem. If it is a 1,000-word feature, however, you will need to make drastic cuts. This involves skill, but it is a skill well worth acquiring.

If you want to know whether you can edit for the web, try the following exercise. Take your best piece of long copy – say, a 1,000-word feature. Make sure it is something you are perfectly happy with; something you would not change a word of. Now cut it down to 500 words.

This is on the outer limits of what you could get away with on a website. A content editor would probably want to break up the copy a bit to make it easier to read online. Now, try cutting it down to just 250 words. In the process, you will have to ditch virtually all your fancy prose. Your argument will be reduced to the bare skeleton of what you want to say. You will have no option but to get to the point. This copy will be fine for the web.

What if you cannot reduce the text that far? Is there a critical example or argument that is eating up space on the page? If so, try cutting it out and placing it on a different page, with a link to the main text. This is the way you need to think about copy on the web. Each piece of text must be short; but a chain of texts can go on forever.

Content editors have to take a similarly critical eye to all the material that comes in, hacking away at it to create the screen-sized blocks that join together to form each website.

3. The Appearance of Text

Because of the difficulties associated in reading and moving around web text, style and layout can be of critical importance to good website design and copy readability. Even if you are not in charge of how your text will look on screen, it is important to have an understanding of the constraints on layout imposed by the online medium so you can take them into account when drafting material.

Hyperlinks

Internet users move around via channels known as hyperlinks, which can be embedded in almost any element of a web page: a picture, an area, a sentence or a word. When used in text, HTML usually indicates that the link is there by colouring the text blue and underlining it. In a well-designed web page, these blue/underline sections stand out so that the reader can see at a glance where the links to other pages are.

The blue/underline convention is not universal; HTML allows programmers to state what style they want hyperlinks to appear in. On my site, for example, I have used a different style for the links in the standard navigation bar down the left-hand side of the page.

However, most web users recognise blue or underlined sections of text as being links. This can make it very confusing if the text is not a link, but has simply been underlined or coloured blue for emphasis.

So the first rule of web copy formatting is: lay off underscores and blue lettering.

Navigation

In the early days of the internet, web designers rapidly recognised that internet users needed all the help they could get in finding their way around. Hence they started using words, such as 'next', 'previous' or 'click here for more', to signpost the way.

This use of copy works after a fashion, but is inelegant for a couple of reasons:

◆ Using signs like 'next' or 'previous' in a chain of pages does not mean much to a visitor who arrives via a link from a page that is not in the chain. Instead, give each page a descriptive subhead that is also a link and provide a list of the subheads on each page.

◆ Using signs like 'click here for x' or 'select this' is wasteful and clumsy when hyperlinks can be incorporated into the text itself. Instead of saying 'The report says x' then 'Click here for the full report', try just 'The report says . . .' If you use context-sensitive links such as these, however, always make sure the reader can easily get back to the point they originally came from, particularly if the new text opens in a new window where the 'back' button on a browser will not lead anywhere.

Other points

When formatting text on screen:

◆ Put line breaks between paragraphs to show clearly where they begin and end.

◆ Lay out text in narrow columns to make it easier for the eye to follow each line. Ideally, a text column should not take up more than a third of the width of a screen, but bear in mind that different types of screen have different sizes.

◆ Use (but do not over-use) bold and italic fonts to help particular points stand out and make it easier for the reader to keep their eye fixed on a paragraph while scrolling down the page.

◆ Make sure the colour of the text will enable it to stand out from its background (so dark letters out of pale backgrounds and vice versa).

4. Thinking in Hypertext

Because of the way it is all inter-linked, the internet can be viewed as one gigantic document, the components of which can be accessed and read in any order.

The components of this single, non-linear text are known in the business as hypertexts and an awareness of hypertext structure is important if you are to add more material to what is already on the web.

Hypertext's two main features are that it usually comprises small, distinct documents (such as web pages) stored electronically, and these documents are linked to each other in a variety of ways. Thus, if you are planning to write for the web, you need to consider not just how you will break up your text but also how you will link its constituent parts to each other and to other web-based documents.

The first task is fairly straightforward. Take your subject matter and break it down to headings and subheadings until you have reduced it to chunks of around one or two screens' worth in length. These are your individual web pages.

Next, however, you need to think about the interconnections between them and make sure these are clearly marked in your copy. To do this, look at your pages and check to see where there are cross-references between them, or where such cross-references could usefully be introduced. Also, are there other links you could include, say to other websites? How many links you can include on a page is really up to the structure of the site and your own ingenuity. The average page should include at least a couple, however.

One common, and very handy, type of link is what is called a 'mailto'; instead of connecting the reader to another web page, it automatically opens up a blank email with a pre-determined address. Use it, for example, wherever you mention the words 'contact us' on a website.

Copy considerations

A consequence of hypertext is that it is difficult to govern which part of a website a reader will arrive at first. Logic dictates they will come via the home page, but that need not necessarily be the case if another website owner decides to create a link to one of the other pages you are creating.

As a result, you need to write every page as a stand-alone document that will make sense to someone who has no knowledge of the rest of the site. This can partly be achieved with headlines and subheads.

A headline on each page that reads 'Company X: leaders in supply chain software' will give newcomers a good idea of the kind of site they have arrived at, for example. At the same time, though, your body copy needs to be a complete text: introduce the subject, expand on it and then finish with a closing line, which should usually be a call to action ('contact us' with a mailto).

> **Do not forget, that you can make your text more succinct by taking out examples, definitions and so on and putting them on other pages, connected to the first via hyperlinks.**

5. Words To Watch Out For

Early websites were almost entirely written by geeks, who tend to speak a peculiar version of English which is riddled with acronyms and buzzwords. As a result, web copy as we know it was born with a range of common phrases, such as 'check out', that have quickly become hackneyed and over-used.

Early web speak also had a tendency to relate to the underlying architecture of sites rather than their content, which may have been interesting to other web designers but certainly not to a general audience. Hence the common use on the internet of phrases such as 'check out this web page'. (What would you make of the line 'check out this page' in a printed publication?)

So watch out for (and avoid) phrases like:

◆ check out

◆ click (as in 'click here')

◆ come back often

◆ cool

◆ current

◆ cutting edge

◆ feel free

◆ surf

◆ view.

> **For a fuller list of words to be avoided (with the reasons why),
> look up Jutta Degener's Dangerous Words at
> http://kbs.cs.tu-berlin.de/~jutta/ht/writing/words.html.**

6. Other Essential Information

There is a number of features of web publishing which are well worth knowing about even though they are not directly related to text, if for no other reason than they could save you from embarrassment when discussing internet sites with clients or business partners.

Images

Unlike text, images use up a lot of memory in a computer and, because of that, typically take longer to download when viewed on an internet site. This can increase the time it takes for a web page to appear on screen and, theoretically, put people off visiting a site.

The critical memory size that a web page can go up to used to be around

32 kilobytes; this used to be the amount of information that would take a second or so to download using an average modem. Nowadays, modem speeds have increased (dramatically so in the case of broadband), but it is still good practice to keep the total size of each web page as low as possible. Reducing the size of images is a good way of doing this.

'Reducing the size', however, does not necessarily refer to the physical dimensions of an image on the screen. A more effective way of cutting down on the amount of memory space a picture uses up is to decrease its resolution. Resolution equates to the sharpness of an image and is measured in dots-per-inch, or dpi. Images in glossy magazines usually need to have a resolution of at least 300dpi, but the resolution of a computer screen is much less than this – typically 72dpi. Consequently, any image that has a resolution of more than 72dpi and is being used on a website is simply using up memory space for no good reason.

Another way to reduce the size of an image file is to store it in a format that does a good job of packing lots of information into very little space. Two formats are commonly used for this purpose on the web. The first, usually called a jpeg or jpg (the file suffix for the format, which was developed by the Joint Photographic Experts Group), is good at storing photos. The second, called gif (for Graphics Interchange Format), is good for storing other image types such as diagrams. Animated gifs can be used to store animation sequences, and have become the standard for online banner ads.

> **So the golden rule with online images is that they should be in jpeg or gif format, have a resolution of around 72dpi and a file size of no more than around 30 kilobytes.**

Meta-tags

Besides the copy and images that you see on screen, HTML allows for each web page to have texts that are invisible to the viewer but can be read by the web browser and other internet applications. These texts, known as meta-tags, have various purposes. One type provides the text that appears in the title bar at the top of the browser window. Another provides a description of the page that can be used by search engines in providing results of a keyword search. Yet another provides the keywords themselves that will allow a search engine to match the page to a search.

Finally, there is a form of tag – the image tag – which is seen by website visitors whenever a cursor passes over a tagged image. This kind of tag can be likened to a photo caption, albeit one that has to be activated by an action on the part of the viewer.

These meta-tags need to be created by someone (although there are programs that can create them automatically) and therefore can be seen as an extension of the copywriting you are doing elsewhere on a site. If you want or are asked to include meta-tags in your web copy, bear in mind the following:

◆ Title tags need to be descriptive: 'Bloggs Co specialist widget engineering' rather than simply an unhelpful 'Bloggs Co' or 'Bloggs Co website'.

◆ Search engines use description tags as the précis of a page, so they need to give a brief account of the contents and sell them to potential visitors. I usually write them almost in the style of small ads.

◆ Keyword tags provide information which search engines use to match pages against search requests. This is not the only information they use; they also match against words in the headline and text. However, since most of the words on any given web page can be found on hundreds, if not thousands, of other pages, keyword tags provide a way of ensuring a unique match to a search phrase. (Or, at least, one that is unique enough to appear fairly high up on a list of search results.) So, when drafting keyword tags, think of words and phrases that are relevant to your web page and could be entered by someone looking for the site, but are not shared by thousands of other sites. On a technology site, for example, the keyword 'software' will do no more than ensure your page ends up somewhere near the end of a list of about two million. Instead, try something specific, such as 'software for customer relationship management.' To find out whether a particular phrase is already used by a large number of other sites, simply key it into a search engine and see how many results it returns.

◆ Image tags are not only displayed if a cursor moves over the picture, but also if the picture cannot be displayed. Therefore they need to be more descriptive than standard picture captions: 'A photo of Company X chief executive Fred Bloggs', for example.

Flash

Adobe Flash is a program that allows web designers to incorporate sophisticated animation sequences into websites. It is loved by designers because it allows them to show off three-dimensional and animation design skills, and generally makes websites look much more, er, flashy than HTML. However, flash pages cannot be read by search engines and have historically not been able to carry meta tags either, so the points above that are to do with helping search engines find a particular page are to a certain extent void if you are dealing with a Flash site. In fact, if your client is building a Flash site they would be well advised to create a mirror site in HTML.

14

Writing for the Press

1. A Major Market

Press represents, without a doubt, the single biggest market for writers in the UK, with an output which exceeds that of advertising or any other marketing-related discipline. The main problem for copywriters in trying to crack this market is that it is already well served by a highly organised and qualified body of professionals – known as journalists.

In order to compete, commercial copywriters not only need to be good at crafting text, but also to have first-rate research skills, an appreciation of legal aspects of publishing and a knack for writing stories to any given length.

This is not to say, however, that journalistic writing cannot be a valuable source of income for independent copywriters. Essentially there are two ways in which you can exploit this market for profit:

◆ You can write directly for papers, magazines or websites, under the aegis of the editor, and be paid directly by the publication.

◆ You can write articles on behalf of your clients, for placement in the press. This, strictly speaking, is public relations, which is covered in more detail in the next chapter.

When considering writing for the press, bear in mind that pay scales vary widely from one publication to another, but are almost always lower than for commercial projects. A good average magazine or newspaper rate would be between £200 and £250 per thousand words – around two-thirds of what you might charge for the same amount of marketing copy.

Throughout this chapter I refer to 'press' as newspapers and magazines, although the same principles extend to the online versions of most publications. I have opted not to cover radio or television at all in this chapter, since they are two types of media which provide only rare opportunities for commercial copywriters.

2. The Principles of Journalism

In addition to the principles of good copywriting covered in Chapter 8, journalism usually involves a degree of *reporting*. Reporting has a number of features which set it apart from other types of writing; the most obvious are the following.

Newsworthiness

Information has to be newsworthy to be of value. This newsworthiness is usually determined by an editor, who will judge it on the following criteria:

◆ Is the information relevant and interesting to the audience of the publication?

◆ Is it recent enough to qualify as 'news'? (Note that the definition of 'recent' varies according to how often a publication comes out.)

◆ Is it exclusive or has it been covered elsewhere? (Unless an event has national importance, editors will often not be interested in covering it without an exclusive angle.)

Authenticity

Reporters deal in facts. Getting facts right is arguably the most important part of a reporter's job. If the facts are wrong, the story is at best worthless and at worst potentially very damaging, as so many high-profile libel cases testify. This has several profound implications for writers:

◆ It is your duty to make sure every single fact that you state is correct. This includes name spellings, job titles, dates, times, amounts, sources and quotes. Become proficient at making notes (or, better still, learn shorthand) and check all information you are not 100 per cent certain of. In the worst-case scenario, you may have to stand up and defend it in court.

◆ You have to become good at using language to convey subtle implied meanings that can help a story stand up in the absence of facts. For example, the phrase 'So-and-so is believed to be . . .' implies that there is good reason to report an event (perhaps an off-the-record confirmation, for example), but no hard facts. The critical thing here is that the reader is still informed but the authenticity of the story is not compromised if the information turns out to be wrong. Many journalistic terms (such as 'poised to', 'looking to' and so on) work in this way and so should not be used simply as stylistic devices.

◆ The requirement for authenticity does not stop with checking your own facts. You need to check existing facts, too, to make sure they are correct in the first place. Despite every journalist's best efforts to get things right, time and other constraints can often conspire to create errors in reporting that then go on to be taken as factually correct. From my experience in both the press and public relations industries, I would say it was not unusual for up to 30 per cent of an average story to be wrong, including, sometimes, the very basis it was founded on.

Independence

Since reporting needs to be truthful, most publications go to great lengths to remain independent of corporate influences that could put a slant on stories. So, unlike other types of copywriting, where it is almost obligatory for your client and anyone else involved to approve your text, press editors are likely to take a dim view of any input from third parties outside the paper or magazine you are writing for, on the basis that such input is likely to introduce bias and damage the integrity of the story.

This freedom from interference is undoubtedly one of the big attractions of journalism, but it greatly increases the need to check and double-check facts at source.

Another consequence of the press's independent stance is that, as a writer, you are obliged (or at least supposed) to provide a balance of opinions in each story. So, for example, if you are writing about a brand new consumer product, you should seek the opinions of a user as well as those of the company behind the launch.

3. The Editorial Process

All newspaper and magazine stories follow a clear-cut process before they appear in print. The following steps are shared by virtually all publications.

◆ A story lead is logged. This could come from an outside agency (such as a press release), a fact uncovered by the writer/journalist, or an idea from the editor.

◆ The editor weighs up the story lead against the other leads for the issue and decides whether or not to proceed with it.

◆ The editor logs the story on a draft page plan and gives a brief, for example covering the number of words needed and a rough idea of the angle, to the journalist/writer.

◆ The journalist/writer researches the story and writes up a draft.

◆ The editor checks the draft and if necessary changes its position on the page plan. The journalist/writer may be asked to re-write the story if more or fewer words are needed for it to fit in its allocated place on the page.

◆ The draft then goes to a sub-editor who checks it for factual and grammatical accuracy. Sub-editors (frequently abbreviated to 'subs') are the people on newspapers and magazines who are in charge of taking raw copy and presenting it on the page for sign-off by the editor. Copy subs check stories for style and accuracy; layout subs handle page design and write headlines and captions.

◆ On most small and medium-sized publications, the copy and layout subbing jobs are combined, so the same sub will be responsible for checking and laying out the story on the page.

◆ Once the page has been put together, it is checked by the production editor and again by the editor.

◆ The page is sent off for printing, at which point no further changes can be made.

> This process usually only varies depending on the number of people involved. On a very small publication, for example, the editor may carry out the functions of writer, sub-editor and production editor. On a large national newspaper, each section will have its own editor and there may even be page editors beneath them; sub-editing will be split between copy and layout subs; and so on.

4. Sources of Information

One of the key skills you need to develop in order to write for the press is to be able to uncover information. Like TV detectives, every journalist normally has a network of contacts that they can call upon for leads, clarification and corroboration, and so on. They also rely heavily on in-house resources like cuttings libraries that can bring up all previous coverage on a subject in a matter of minutes.

If you are involved only in the occasional piece of press writing and are doing it from your normal workplace rather than at the offices of the publication in question, it is unlikely you will have access to either the resources or the networks used by other journalists. Nevertheless, there is still a couple of perfectly good research tools at your disposal. First of all, an internet search will give you information on relevant organisations and any widely-reported news to date. Secondly, both the phone book and the *Yellow Pages* can be invaluable in providing contact numbers that will act as a starting point for your investigations. If you are based outside London, it is probably worth getting hold of both directories for the capital because of the number of global businesses that have their headquarters there. You can also access directory enquiries online, although I find the paper directories are often easier to work with if you know what you are looking for.

Following up story leads, or developing feature ideas, is often a bit like working your way through an Agatha Christie murder mystery. You may well have one or two preconceived ideas regarding your subject matter, but your conversations with sources should help lead you towards a more truthful picture of what is going on. Remember that you are aiming for a balanced, accurate view. Speak to as many people as necessary to get that view. And make sure that you have made notes to back it up along the way.

How many people do you need to speak to?

Getting to the bottom of a story can take no time at all, or as much time as you can possibly spare. It all depends on the length of the copy and, usually, the importance of the subject you are writing about.

A new product launch that is being written up as a filler story can sometimes be despatched in a couple of lines culled from a press release. A typical news story, say of a couple of hundred words, may merit one or two phone calls if the information you need is fairly easy to come by. When writing a feature, however, you may wonder how much research is needed before you can be satisfied that you have come up with a well-rounded picture of your subject matter. Again, it can vary from one single interview (for example, if you are doing a profile piece) to up to a dozen or more for an investigative feature. One thing you need to be aware of is that the research for any given article is likely to take just as long as, if not longer than, the time it takes to write up the story.

You will also come across different levels of willingness to help, depending on your subject matter. As a general (and hardly surprising) rule, individuals and businesses that stand to gain from exposure in the article will normally be relatively keen to help. However, if your subject matter is sensitive in any way then you will need to allow for a degree of resistance from your contacts. I once had the bright idea of writing about layoffs for a magazine around about the time of the dotcom crash but, after getting the commission, found it nigh impossible to get anyone in business to talk openly about the subject.

5. Writing News

I believe news reporting is a good grounding for other types of writing because it teaches you the most basic lesson of good copy: make your point straightaway and make it clearly. This does not mean that the best news reporters are great writers. On one level, the most fundamental skill in news generation is being able to gather the facts which tell a story that nobody else has been able to uncover.

Nevertheless, writing is a fundamental part of the process and even though news reporters may not necessarily have to worry about perfect prose, they do often need to deliver extremely tight copy to demanding deadlines. Besides turning in your copy on time, if you are working on or with a news desk it is important to make sure your stories follow a structure that allows them to be cut from the bottom.

> **A good rule of thumb when editing your own material is that your story should always make sense when you chop the last paragraph out – no matter how many times you repeat the process.**

6. Writing Features

Feature writing generally pays better than news and provides greater opportunities for creative expression. You can pick your subject matter, although if you write regularly for a publication you may find the editor suggests topics for you to follow up. And the deadlines tend to be more lax. In fact, you may have so much freedom with feature writing that one of the biggest problems can be to know where to start and finish your text.

To an extent, your narrative will be dictated by the type of feature you are writing. Most features fall into clearly defined categories – for example, personal profiles, investigations, industry reports and so on – whose style can be assessed by reference to a few back issues of the magazine you are writing for.

Where to start

That still, however, can leave you wondering how to kick off your feature in the absence of a strong news hook.

My first piece of advice would be to look back through your notes and see if there is anything that stands out, such as a statistic, a quote or an anecdote.

Some classic ways to start a feature are:

◆ Start small then go large. Use an individual example or case study as the introduction to your general subject matter. For example: 'Fisherman Bill Bundy remembers a time when there were so many cod in the sea you could pick them out with your hands. He gave up fishing this season, affected, along with thousands of others, by a massive crash in stocks that could see the species driven to extinction . . .'

◆ Start large then go small. Focus on a general trend for your introduction and then back it up with examples. For example: 'Thousands of fishermen gave up their nets this year following a massive crash in cod stocks. Bill Bundy, one of those affected, remembers when . . .'

◆ Start with a quote. This practice is greatly over-used and generally frowned upon by editors, and should never be used in news stories. Sometimes, however, a strong quote can provide just enough of a hook to justify its use in a feature intro. For example: ' "I never expect to see a cod again in my life," says fisherman Bill Bundy . . .'

◆ Pose a question. This can be a good way of beginning a feature as long as you answer it. For example: 'What is the fastest-dwindling fish in the sea? For the answer, look no further than your local chip shop . . .'

Other tips on structure

Once you have worked out how to begin your feature, your next two aims should be to make sure it flows well and that it gets a point across.

This is where some back-of-a-cigarette-packet planning can help. First of all, based on your research, work out what the conclusion of your feature will be. Then, look at all the supporting and contradictory evidence and arrange it in a logical sequence to construct a coherent argument.

> **When writing, make one point per paragraph and support it where possible with data or a quote. This one-point-per-paragraph structure will help if you or your editor need to change the order of the information around.**

Use of quotes

In general, use quotes to support the points you make in the text. For example: 'Nobody knows if cod stocks will bounce back. "We just do not have enough data on breeding habits," said one marine biologist . . .'

7. Headlines and Captions

In most situations, headlines and captions get written for you. Occasionally, however, you may have to write them yourself, for example if you are working with a small-circulation magazine or employee newsletter (see Chapter 12) with few in-house subbing resources. Here is what you need to know about each.

Headlines

Try to distil your story down to just a few words, including an active verb. For example: 'Fishermen reel as cod stocks plunge'. This example has the added advantage of including a double meaning or pun, which may or may not be appropriate depending on the overall style and tone of the publication. It also breaks neatly over two lines of text or 'decks':

Fishermen reel as

cod stocks plunge

Being able to break the copy in this way is important as headlines often take up more than a single deck on the page. The ideal headline will break equally well over one, two or three decks and will be easy to cut from the bottom. Here is a variation of our previous example, to illustrate the point:

Fishing stops

in cod slump

across the UK

Each line adds information to the one before it and can be chopped out without rendering the headline meaningless.

Captions

Check the caption style used in the publication you are writing for. Many use an introductory adjective as a way of grabbing the reader's attention; for example: 'Endangered – North Sea cod'. In any event, the caption should serve two purposes: to inform the reader and entice them to read more. Obviously, then, it needs to describe what is going on in the picture, but it also needs to get across something interesting or newsworthy. Finally, it needs to fit in the space under the picture. Which, in the case of a head-and-shoulders shot, can be very small indeed.

> **If you are supplying images with your copy and need to write a caption for use by a layout sub later on, try to include as much information as possible.**

8. Writing To Length

Being able to produce the right amount of text is an important skill in any area of copywriting, but it is particularly critical in newspapers and magazines because space on the page is at a premium. Running over your word count by a paragraph or two would not be a problem on a website, for example, but on a newspaper or magazine it would create headaches for production staff and you could end up losing material that you felt was vital to your story.

To avoid running over, the best option is to keep an eye on your word count once you get about halfway through your story. Aim to over-run slightly in your first draft, say by about five per cent, and then go back and edit the whole story down to the right length. I usually aim to hand in copy that is within plus or minus five words of the target word count. This may be a bit pedantic if you are writing a major article, but if you find your draft is more than about five per cent longer than it should be (say, 50 words over on a 1,000-word feature), perhaps you should think about losing a paragraph somewhere.

There may also be times, particularly when writing news stories, that there simply is not enough information to hand to stretch the article to the length you need. Your options then are to try to extend the scope of the story, for example by bringing in more background information, or to let your editor know as soon as possible so they can adjust the page plan accordingly.

9. Writing for Newspapers, Magazines, Contract Publishers and News Wires

The differences in approach that you will come across in working for different types of journalistic media are mainly to do with the kinds of deadlines you will encounter and the number of people you will work with. Taking each of the major outlets for press writing in turn . . .

Newspapers

Tend to be at least weekly in frequency and will often have a relatively large number of in-house writers, although a large amount of content is also bought in from agencies and stringers (freelance writers who act as correspondents for the paper). The editorial agenda is usually driven by news and there may be several deadlines in a single day for different editions of the paper.

Features desks operate at a (slightly) more leisurely pace and tend to farm out more of their work. It is normal for different columnists and contributing editors to 'own' a page or section of the paper and produce most of the material for it.

Magazines

These tend to be at most weekly in frequency and have relatively few in-house editorial staff. On features-based magazines it is not unusual for practically all the stories to be commissioned from freelance writers.

Rates tend to be better than for newspapers. When pitching stories, however, bear in mind that pictures can be an important part of the subject matter; you may need to make sure images are available to go with your text.

Contract publishers

Contract publishing is the term for customer magazines produced by publishers under contract from the owners of well-known brands. It includes in-flight and supermarket magazines, for example.

From humble beginnings, contract publishing has grown into a major industry which deserves an entire book to itself. Some of the highest-circulation magazines in the UK are contract-published titles and virtually every major magazine publisher now has a contract arm, competing with dozens of specialist firms that have hitherto dominated the sector.

Customer magazines tend to operate along lines that are essentially a mix of magazine publishing and internal communications (see Chapter 12). Each title has a small number of editorial staff, with a large amount of material being farmed out to freelance writers, but there is also a level of editorial input and control from the client.

Frequency tends to be no more than monthly and so deadlines are correspondingly long. Expect rates to be roughly on a par with those in the traditional magazine sector, although there may be room for negotiation if the client feels you can contribute specialist knowledge.

News wires

News wires and agencies provide much of the news that goes into 'the news'. Pick up any paper and if you spot a by-line that says 'staff reporter', it is more than likely that the story came from an agency such as Reuters or Associated Press. Although many of the larger agencies have features departments, the daily story agenda is likely to be almost completely news-driven. Most editorial staff work in-house or under contract and information tends to be published as soon as it has been written up, so there are no deadlines as such. Rates tend to be modest compared with, say, the magazine sector.

10. Pitching Ideas

Unlike other forms of copywriting, where there usually has to be a ready need and budget for you to get a job, it is possible to sell a significant amount of work to editors simply by pitching speculative ideas. The process for doing this is relatively straightforward. Pick a publication, pick a subject, do some research on it, and contact the editor with your proposal for a story. It can be a good idea to phone up the editorial department in the first place, although an editor will almost always ask to see a synopsis by letter, fax or email.

Your synopsis should be a short summary of the story you intend to write (usually not more than about 100 to 150 words), mentioning the sources you have approached or are hoping to approach for information. Also include notes on photography (if there is any), a line or two on your credentials as a writer, contact details and possibly a specimen introduction.

Your chances of success with any pitch will be greatly improved if you have a good feel for the publication and have picked a subject that is likely to appeal to its readers. Getting a foot in the door can often take a lot of perseverance, as editors usually prefer to work with freelancers that they know and trust. But once you build up a relationship with an editor you may well become a regular contributor to the publication.

15

Writing for Public Relations

1. The Difference Between Journalism and PR

To the uninitiated, public relations (or PR) might seem to have a lot in common with journalism. Both are ostensibly concerned with providing the public with truthful facts, predominantly by means of written words in the media. Both focus on 'news'. And in many cases, the output from the two industries – press releases in the case of PR and news stories in the case of journalism – appear to be very similar or even identical.

However, the truth to those who work in either industry (and I have worked in both) is that PR and journalism sit uneasily together, each usually viewing the other as something of a necessary evil. The press derives a good part of its daily news from the activities of businesses and rich or famous individuals and these, in turn, resort to PR to both exploit the opportunities this presents and provide protection from over-exploitation by the media. Journalists view this protectionism as needless interference. PR practitioners, meanwhile, resent the fact that they have to rely on news coverage to do their job, particularly since press attention on their clients never seems to be greater than when a disaster has just occurred. The key difference between both parties is really one of allegiance. PR officers (often abbreviated to PROs or PRs) have a clearly-stated objective to portray their clients in the best possible light at all times. Journalists have a somewhat woollier duty to provide their readerships with accurate information, but in reality are often mainly concerned with producing headlines (hence the only half-joking phrase 'Never let the truth get in the way of a good story'). Given the choice between the PR and press versions of the same story, I would hesitate to say which is likely to be the more accurate and truthful; the only thing that can be said with certainty is that the press story is likely to be more balanced, although it may well contain biases which are not obvious.

Outlets for writing

The PR industry's output is measured almost entirely in words; not just words of coverage in the press, but also in the text used to secure that coverage (such as news releases and press packs) and even in the reports, proposals and briefing documents that accompany the process. It is not unusual for the latter, in fact, to make up the bulk of the output from agencies and in-house teams, with relatively little effort being devoted to press materials. What is more, the number of trained writers in the PR industry is not very large, so writing skills are at a premium. The upshot is that PR offers great opportunities for writers with a strong news sense. Ex-journalists, in particular, tend to be valued by agencies and in-house teams alike. However, it has to be said that the industry does not favour all temperaments. It is not unusual for some press materials to go through months of re-writes, often to the detriment of the finished product, and those involved on the writing side may need to be able to keep their cool in the face of pedantic, spurious and grammatically inept corrections.

> The fees you charge for PR writing can easily be a third or so higher than equivalent work in the press. However, bear in mind when quoting that a lot of PR work eats up time like nothing else. You can easily agree on what you think is an astronomical figure for a fairly straightforward job and end up feeling underpaid when the work drags on for days or weeks. To get round this, either quote on a day-rate basis or stipulate a cut-off point after which further work will incur extra charges.

2. How PR Works

The International Committee of Public Relations Consultancies Associations describes public relations as 'the managed process of communication between one group and another'. The aim of most PR programmes, however, is usually simply to improve the portrayal of a business or individual (the client) in the media.

This improvement can be in terms of the number of mentions or the way the client is mentioned. If a client is getting a lot of bad press, for example, the main task for PR may well be to put a lid on all coverage for a while. In most cases, however, the objective (and the basis for campaign measurement) is the increase in the number of positive mentions a client gets in the press. This usually involves a process along the following lines.

◆ The client retains or recruits a PR practitioner or team of practitioners. Large businesses tend to have an in-house PR team, while smaller companies and individuals may employ an agency or a freelance professional. It is also not unusual for in-house teams to employ the services of a PR agency, either to cope with work peaks or, more usually, to undertake specific projects.

◆ The client briefs the PR practitioner or team on their objectives. Beyond simply getting more mentions in the press, for example, they may be keen to promote a particular product or to raise sales in a specific area.

◆ The PR practitioner or team proposes measures that can meet the client's objectives by improving the way they are portrayed in the media. There is a vast array of potential ways of garnering media coverage, ranging, for example, from sponsoring an industry awards event to taking journalists out to lunch to talk to them about the state of the widget market (or whatever).

◆ Those measures that are deemed most appropriate to the client's brief and budget will go on to form the basis for one or several PR campaigns.

◆ The PR practitioner or team then sets about preparing the materials that will be used as the background for coverage. These can include press releases, information packs and so on.

◆ Once the materials have been approved they are distributed to the press, usually along with invitations to face-to-face or telephone briefings.

◆ The resulting coverage is collected and measured in terms of quantity and quality. Most PR programmes measure the number of times a particular take-out or 'key message' (such as 'company X is the leading widget company in the country') is mentioned.

3. Giving Journalists the Basis of a Story

A common misconception held by many in the public relations industry and elsewhere is that PR provides the press with stories.

This is baloney.

PR provides the press with the *basis* for stories. That basis can be a news announcement, a briefing or a new product launch, for example. (For that matter, a product or company's failure to live up to its PR hype can also form the basis of a story.) The fact is, though, that no self-respecting editor is going to value a sheet of information that he or she knows for a fact has been sent to dozens or even hundreds of rival publications.

At best, the press release can serve as a trigger for a reporter to uncover something a bit more exclusive. This has important implications for how press releases and other press materials should be drafted. One agency head, a former boss of mine, best summed up the approach by saying that the art of PR consisted in trying to trick journalists into believing they had stumbled across a story. With that in mind, let's move on to what is involved.

4. Writing a Damn Good Press Release

The angle

◆ First of all, what is the brief for the story? And, more importantly, is it interesting? Get hold of some of the magazines or papers the client wants to get coverage in and see if you can imagine this story being given space in them.

◆ If you are lucky, you may find there is a ready-made slot for the kind of news your client is touting. Many trade magazines, for example, have appointments columns where you can place stories about the latest corporate-climbing exploits in your client's business.

◆ If that is the case, write your announcement in a style that closely resembles the slot it will go into. Use a similar word count to make the editor's job as easy as possible. But include as much supplementary information as you can, in a 'Notes to editors' section (see below).

◆ If you are even luckier, your client's announcement may be important enough to qualify as real news in its own right. The client may have discovered the secret of nuclear fusion, for example, or invented a way to stop toast falling with the buttered side down. If this is the case, your intro should tell the story as simply and succinctly as possible. But it is rarely the case.

◆ More often than not, press releases are of the form: 'Company X is pleased to announce its new line of widgets'. Announcements of such earth-shattering insignificance will usually be lucky to make it to the waste-paper bin, let alone the front page. Before you sit down to write a straight release on anything of this ilk, consider the following. Companies need to launch new products to stay in business. They are supposed to win contracts. They are expected to form partnerships. In fact, most of what your client may claim is 'news' is actually to do with things that the business should be doing anyway. So why would it be remotely interesting to an editor?

◆ If your announcement is one of the 99.9 per cent of announcements that fall into this category, you need to look for ways to elevate it beyond the ordinary. Lateral thinking can help here. Is there an angle to what your client is doing that is quite unusual? Is it an industry or market first, or last, or biggest, or smallest? Will the announcement have wider repercussions? One of the reasons I used cod as an example in the previous chapter is because I once had to elevate a story about the fish in some work I did for WWF, the global environment network. The story was actually about a new campaign to raise awareness of falling stocks, which in itself was not big news (since campaigning is what organisations like WWF are supposed to do). So, to make it more relevant to the public, I proposed an announcement placing cod 'n' chips, one of Britain's national dishes, on the endangered species list. There was some poetic licence involved, of course, since a menu item cannot technically be declared an endangered species, but WWF went along with the conceit and the resulting release was interesting enough to editors to make the story an agenda item the day it went out.

Style and content

◆ Once you have nailed your angle, if it is a good one, you may be tempted to use all sorts of *Sun*-style puns in your headline and introduction. Don't. Remember, your press release is not the story; it is the background to a story. Leave all the clever word-play to the journalists. The one thing they hate worse than a PR is a wise-guy PR. Simply spell out your story with an intro of 25 words or less, using words of no more than three syllables. That takes a lot more skill than writing any number of puns.

◆ Also avoid using phrases such as 'thought to' or 'poised to' for purely stylistic purposes. While the press is at liberty to report on speculation and rumour, the purpose of a press release is to impart facts.

◆ Next, back up your intro with as much information as you think can be possibly relevant. Include facts, figures, amounts, dates, locations and references. Again, stick to simple words and short sentences. One point per sentence or paragraph, in order of decreasing importance.

◆ Make sure the salient points are easy to read and can be picked out simply by scanning the copy. Use bullet points or numbered lists where they will help with clarity.

Page numbers and quotes

◆ If your press release is more than one page long, indicate that there is a second page with 'cont . . .' for 'continued', 'm/f' for 'more follows' or '1/2' for one page out of two. Some press releases still get faxed to editors, who will need to know if one of the pages has got lost.

◆ If your press release is more than two pages long, look again to see if you have included too much information. Most busy editors will not plough beyond the first page anyway. If necessary, take some of the less interesting stuff out of the main body of the release and include it as background in bullet points on the final sheet.

◆ All press releases should carry a quote from a named (and titled) spokesperson, but leave it until the end of the press release. Nine times out of ten, a journalist will try to speak to someone directly to get an original quote, so the purpose of the quote in the press release is simply to provide a backup.

◆ Make sure, nevertheless, that the quote bears at least some vague resemblance to spoken English. Many press release quotes end up full of marketing-speak or techno-babble and cannot even be used as a backup.

Finishing off

◆ At the end of the story, write 'Ends' and centre it on the page so that it is obvious. If you do not, some poor editorial assistant could end up hunting around the fax machine looking for another sheet of paper (and they won't thank you for it).

◆ Then include the names, phone numbers and email addresses of at least two people who can be contacted for more information. (Email addresses are optional; phone numbers are not.)

◆ There is a good argument for including these contact details on the first page, too, if space and layout will permit.

◆ There may be information which is not relevant to your story but which needs to be included for legal reasons, or to conform to house style; many companies insist on a short paragraph, called a 'boilerplate', which describes their business and is unchanged from one press release to another. This information should be included in bullet points under the heading 'Notes to editors', at the end of the main release. Feel free to include as much background information in this section as you like; it can often come in handy when a journalist needs to pad out a story.

> **If the story is embargoed for a particular date, make sure you state so clearly, along with the date and time of the embargo, at the top of the first page of your press release.**

5. Key Messages

One of the most important parts of the press release writing process is to make sure that certain key messages are included in the text.

Key messages are statements that, it is hoped, will eventually appear in the press coverage and will help improve the way the client is perceived by the public. Key messages also play a fundamental part in the evaluation of many PR campaigns.

Unfortunately for copywriters, many key messages are dreamt up by marketing committees and tend to be unwieldy to say the least.

Crow-barring key messages into an otherwise tightly-written press statement can be a job in itself; including them in a way which will ensure they get used by journalists can sometimes be well nigh impossible.

If you have the liberty of coming up with key messages yourself, make sure they mirror the brand and are simple, straightforward and flexible. So a key message for Bert's Widgets that reads 'the leading widget manufacturer in the North West' is preferable to 'purveyors of excellence in widget solutions worldwide', for example – no matter what the marketing manager thinks.

If you have to make do with existing key messages, and are finding it hard to fit them into your press release, you can always put them in the client quote. And if it does not get used you can simply blame it on the fact that nine out of ten journalists prefer to get a quote direct from a spokesperson, so it is up to the spokespeople to get the messages across.

6. When Not To Write Press Releases

Remember that a press release is just a starting point for a story, and as far as most editors are concerned it is a pretty poor starting point because they know it has been sent to all their competitors. It therefore stands to reason that there can be other ways of creating a story – and some of them can be just as effective, if not more.

One of the best ways of getting a journalist's attention, in fact, is to tip them off *without* a press release. This implies an exclusive lead, something guaranteed to get any reporter's attention. It also implies the 'news' has not been gestating in some corporate communications department for weeks, so it might actually be worth hearing. Even for an off-the-cuff tip-off, though, it helps to have some written material prepared, whether in the form of a sheet of bullet points or a carefully crafted email.

From a copywriter's perspective, the benefit of using this method is that it can help you steer clear of situations where you think a press release will involve a lot of work with little reward, either for yourself or for the client.

Because they are seen to be official documents, press releases often have to go through immensely complicated approvals procedures and, once released, can lurk in files forever after, with potentially damaging consequences. A backgrounder or tip-off email, on the other hand, can be prepared very easily and might even increase the chances of coverage in the long run.

7. Other Types of Press Material

Although press releases are the mainstay of public relations work, a number of other types of material exists. The most common ones are:

Press packs

The term press pack refers to a collection of information handed out at
events and briefings. It will usually consist of a branded folder, which may or
may not contain copy, plus a press release and photographs.

There may also be other ingredients, such as a company brochure,
product background, CD-ROMs and so on. If you take a brief for a press
pack, the first thing to ascertain is what items will go into it and what the
individual copy requirements will be for each.

Backgrounders

Also called fact-sheets, these are usually one-page documents with
information listed as bullet points. For businesses, backgrounders may
include the number of employees, annual turnover, milestones and so on.
Backgrounders can be easy to put together with some desk research using,
for example, the internet and/or corporate literature such as an annual
statement.

By-lined features

By-lined features usually take the form of opinion pieces attributed to a
senior client and ghost-written by a PR executive or copywriter. The length,
subject matter and tone will often largely be set by the editor of the
publication accepting the piece, but overly commercial messages are
generally to be avoided. Instead, concentrate on researching the relevant
subject matter by means of an interview with a knowledgeable contact in the
client's organisation.

Case studies

Case studies are intended to show a particular service, product or application
in action and are used in a variety of ways. Often they provide useful
background to a story, sometimes they are used to illustrate an article and
sometimes they form the basis of a story on their own.

The exact format for case studies varies from one project to another, but they are usually longer than press releases (between 500 and 1,000 words instead of 250 to 500 for a press release). They also tend to follow a different narrative thread: possibly a summary or introduction, followed by a market overview, a statement of the challenge faced by the business in question, a section on how the challenge was overcome, and a conclusion, possibly ending in a stand-alone quote. If you are taking a brief for this kind of work it is often a good idea to ask the client for examples of the kind of thing they are expecting, so you know how to write it up. Case studies need to have page numbers and contact details, just like press releases.

Picture captions

As its name indicates, the purpose of a picture caption is to provide additional information to go with photography. Since some stories are pitched to picture desks on the strength of images alone, however, PR picture captions need to be much more extensive than those used in the press. In effect, they should be written up as mini press releases, no more than a sheet long but with the same attention to headlines, intros, contacts and so on.

Forward planning notices

The forward planning notice is commonly used to make sure an event is booked into media diaries. Exact styles vary, but to be effective a forward planning notice should be headed as such and obviously needs to include details such as what is happening, when and where. State the nature of the event – press conference, photo call or other – so an editor can assign the right person to cover it, and as always make sure you include the contact details of PR representatives.

Interview opportunities

Interview opportunity notices are predominantly aimed at radio show producers and are effectively a special form of forward planning notice.

The one-page notice should state who is available for interview, why they are worth talking to, when they will be able to go on air, and whether or not they will be available in a studio.

White papers

See the entry in the next chapter.

16

Writing for Sales and Sales Promotion

1. Types of Sales Copy

In this chapter I have lumped together a whole range of types of copywriting that are all more or less directly connected with selling to consumers or businesses (aside from direct marketing, of course, which is covered in Chapter 11). At one end of the spectrum are brochures and leaflets, material which might be considered the classic domain of the marketing copywriter. At the other are specialist documents such as media packs, white papers, point-of-sale (PoS) materials and other types of sales collateral.

The basic rules of good writing (Chapter 8) apply to all these types of projects, just as they do to other copywriting disciplines. The key point of any sales copy is to get straight to the point and bring out benefits, not features, up front.

Here is a brief account of some of the major types of sales promotion work and a few of the copywriting considerations they throw up.

2. Brochures

Historically the mainstay of any sales push, brochures have lost out to websites as a way of reaching out to customers in recent times, but still represent a major potential source of work for professional copywriters. The aim of most brochures is to help in the sales process by providing information, although text is only one element in this. Often much of the take-out from a brochure is subliminal, with high-quality printing, expensive photography and so on all working together to create an image of professionalism that the customer will, ideally, buy into. The design, consequently, is every bit as important as the words. For the copywriter, this usually means brochure projects will involve working closely alongside a designer or, at least, having a good idea of what the layout will look like, and writing to fit in with the themes and word counts dictated by the design.

When taking a brief for a brochure, find out who exactly the publication is aimed at and how it will be used. If possible, talk to the sales force directly to find out what they need to help with their work; it could be a very different animal from that envisaged by, say, the marketing department. If you can, why not go a step further and talk to a few customers, too, to get their views on what will work. On large projects this kind of research may already be factored into the production process.

Check to see what response mechanism needs to be mentioned. Will customers be directed to a website, a freephone number or something similar? And finally, query any information, such as price lists, which might be time-sensitive. Brochures are notoriously costly to produce and your client will not be pleased if their investment is outdated within a few weeks of publication. (For the same reason, be extra careful about checking for mistakes in your copy. You certainly will not be thanked if grammatical or spelling errors crop up in the finished product.)

> **When drafting your copy, keep it as short as possible. Few customers have the time or the inclination to plough through masses of text.**

3. Leaflets, Flyers and Posters

Used above all to promote events, the main ingredients for flyers and posters are a simple, eye-catching headline and an obvious response mechanism. Most of the rest of the copy should be devoted to details such as the date, time, location, the cost of tickets and so on. Since the amount of copywriting involved is minimal, it is hardly worth trying to charge much for this kind of work. It also helps to work alongside a designer.

Leaflets involve more copy but, again, are unlikely to be backed by large budgets. Their production does not normally entail any particular difficulties; as per any other job, be sure to cover any queries in your brief and then write simply and succinctly with your target audience in mind.

4. Point-of-Sale Materials

Point-of-sale (also known in the trade as PoS) is a blanket term for all the posters, stickers, cut-outs, holders and so on that go on and around product stands in a shop. It is an area of crucial importance to the retail industry, since getting customers to buy even one per cent more of a given product can translate to millions of pounds' worth of profits. The main requirements from a copywriting perspective are simple, eye-catching, design-led messages. Space is often at a premium on PoS materials and your message may need to be seen from several feet away, so stick with a few words and write them large.

In your brief, find out what the PoS will look like, how big it will be and how it will be used or positioned in store. Also check whether you need to incorporate special pieces of text, such as terms and conditions.

5. On-Pack

The requirements for on-pack copy are largely dictated by design guidelines and official or regulatory notices, leaving very little margin for creative input. The label on a soft drink, for example, has to accommodate the name of the product, the price, ingredients and nutritional information, plus recycling and disposal logos and other design elements. Even if you are involved at the concept stage, working on product packaging can be fairly frustrating. Something as simple as a name can be hard to pin down because of the number of contenders that have already been registered and, often, the need to test every option through consumer research.

If you are offered this kind of work, my advice would be to always quote on a day-rate basis so that you are covered in the event of the project dragging out over a long period of time.

6. Media Packs

Media packs are used by magazines, newspapers, broadcast stations and websites to sell space to advertisers. Their key function is to provide audience and pricing information so that media planners and buyers will include the title or channel on their advertising schedules. Much of the information, for example on the demographic breakdown of the audience, is best provided in graphic format. For the rest, keep copy to a minimum; media pack readers are ultimately more interested in the figures than in the words. However, it is a good idea to find out during your briefing whether there is anything that sets the publication, channel or site apart from its competitors, and bringing this out in the text.

Confusingly, if you work in PR (see previous chapter), you may find that 'press packs' are sometimes referred to as 'media packs'. Obviously the two are quite different, so make sure you know what you are talking about.

7. Case Studies

Used predominantly in business-to-business pitches, case studies or client references in sales promotion follow roughly the same rules as in PR (see previous chapter). However, given the concerns of the target audience, it is usually more pertinent to cover financial information – how much was saved or gained from using a product, and so on.

8. White Papers

A white paper, in the context of sales collateral, is a quasi-academic essay covering a particular area of industrial development. They are used exclusively in a business-to-business context and usually to promote a technology, format or platform rather than a particular product. Typically they are quite long – up to around 5,000 words – and can be very technical. They are expected to be relatively objective, covering the pros and cons of different options in the area being discussed. Extensive research may be needed in developing a white paper; you will probably want to have access to research, statistics, case studies and so on to make sure that you can write competently about the subject. Break your copy up into sections and include any relevant diagrams you can get your hands on.

9. Dealing With Sales People

Talking to sales people in any organisation can be a very enlightening process because, unlike marketers or staff in any other function, these people are in contact with the customers that keep the business afloat. Taking a brief on any sales promotion or collateral project can give you a real insight into how a company is seen by its customers, which can help you with other projects for the same client or even for projects with other clients in a similar industry sector.

At the same time, however, dealing directly with sales people or teams can be frustrating because they can sometimes have a much less clear idea of what they want to say. Faced with the pressure of always having to meet targets, sales people, one suspects, are tempted to try to fit products into whatever shape a client appears to want, with the end result that they might not always be able to gauge what it is that has attracted the customer to the product in the first place.

Sales people and teams are also very demanding and may require a certain amount of ego-massaging and expectation management. Be clear about timescales, costs, production constraints and so on. Finally, be upfront about how and how much your work can or will benefit them personally – most sales people are ultimately motivated by personal gain.

10. Working With Designers

Since so much of the material described above has a heavy design element, it is worth saying a thing or two at this point regarding designers.

The first thing to know about design is that, compared with copywriting, it is not cheap. Designers charge by the hour and will often work on rates of £700 to £1,000 a day. Furthermore, they effectively have a monopoly over work after it reaches their studios, as only they can make changes to text, images and layout once it is on the page.

What this means in practice is that, for the sake of your client and their budget, you need to ensure as far as possible that all changes to your copy are made *before* it goes off to design. You may well have to educate your clients on this point; many naively assume they can carry on making changes to copy once page layouts start coming through, and then get a nasty shock when the design bill arrives. Clearly, worrying about design budgets should not be a major concern for you unless you are managing the entire project, but avoiding excess design bills can prevent headaches all round and help keep the client happy – a good way of ensuring repeat business.

> **If your work regularly involves a design element, it is worth cultivating a partnership with a design agency so you can offer a 'dual service' to your clients. Conversely, design agencies can be good sources of work in themselves, as they often handle large publishing jobs and rarely have any in-house copywriting resource.**

17

Writing for Other Media

1. An Infinite Variety

In the preceding chapters I have tried to cover the most common types of work you are likely to come across as a copywriter. Each one of these areas would easily merit a book in its own right, and what I have tried to provide are some brief notes on some of the issues you need to bear in mind when approaching the work, rather than an exhaustive guide to each discipline. As you become established you will probably find that most of your work tends to fall into a particular category or set of categories, and you will undoubtedly be keen to learn more by reference to more specialised texts.

In this chapter I cover a number of other potential writing assignments you might encounter. Some of these, such as speech writing and producing technical documents, are important specialist areas in their own right, and tend to be assigned to writers with proven skills rather than mainstream copywriters. Others, such as drafting slide presentations, are of lesser importance in terms of their likely revenue potential. I have listed this diverse group of subjects in alphabetical order.

My personal experience in many of these areas is limited, so what I have to offer by way of advice is more in the form of thoughts and first impressions than hard-and-fast rules. I hope, however, that what follows will be enough to help you go into a brief with a fairly good idea of what to ask and look for. From then on, you should be able to build up a skill base from your own learning.

> **I have tried to make this list as exhaustive as possible, but there is almost no end to the potential kinds of jobs you might be asked to take on as a copywriter. If you are ever stumped for guidance on a particular project, remember that producing simple, succinct and clear copy will almost always meet your client's needs.**

2. Blurbs

The *Pocket Oxford Dictionary* describes a blurb as a 'publisher's (usually eulogistic) description of a book'. In copywriting terms, however, it can mean almost any sort of summary of a larger work that is used for promotional purposes. Its prime purpose is to sell the larger work to interested audiences, so the first job for the writer is to look for messages that will appeal to them.

The sorts of things you might consider include:

◆ an overview ('The first truly comprehensive work of its kind')

◆ excerpts from the work

◆ testimonials from satisfied customers

◆ statements regarding the usefulness or value of the work ('Buy this and watch your profits go through the roof')

◆ or a combination of the above.

When drafting your copy, pay close attention to the length of your text and use emotive words that have immediate appeal for the reader. Avoid jargon and technical terms; bear in mind that the reader will probably give your blurb a couple of seconds' attention, at most, before deciding whether or not to move on. As in many forms of promotional writing, it is not unusual for blurbs to incorporate a measure of artistic licence. How far you go down this route is up to you; in my opinion it is better to concentrate on selling the good points of a poor piece of work than trying to make the entire work out to be something it is not.

Rates for this kind of work tend not to be particularly generous since the amount of copy involved is usually very small. However it can take time to skim through a book or other document in order to produce an informed blurb, so be realistic about what you charge and do not take on projects unless they appear to be worthwhile.

3. Business Plans

A business plan is a short document that companies use to outline their strategies for growth and development. They are useful documents for any management team and are usually the main basis on which outside agencies, such as banks and venture capitalists, will consider funding. Writing or editing business plans can provide another occasional source of copywriting work although you need to be aware that the most critical element of any business plan is not the words it contains, but the figures.

If you are going to do this kind of work, it can help to have written a business plan yourself, perhaps for your own business, and to have presented it to potential partners or backers. If you lack this kind of experience, I would advise talking to your bank manager or someone similar to find out what they like and do not like to see in the business plans they receive. This basic feedback can be very useful in advising clients in start-up businesses or those who have not written a plan before.

If a company is willing to pay for external help in putting together its business plan, it almost always means the document will be used to secure funding, either for a new launch or for business expansion. This means it will be seen exclusively by people who may be in a position to hand over large amounts of cash. These people will be looking, first and foremost, for evidence that they, too, can make money on the deal.

Hence the importance of the figures. An investor is usually looking for a decent return on their money after about three years. In many cases, this return will be by way of a trade sale or public listing. They will therefore want to see tangible evidence that their investment will help the business grow in value, and that it will be secure in the first place.

While the figures should always be put together, or at least checked, by a qualified professional such as an accountant, there is scope for a copywriter to add value elsewhere. If the numbers add up, the potential investor will next look to see whether the business strategy makes sense and is backed by a capable management team. A well-written document can help create an image of professionalism that the investor will feel comfortable about buying into.

If you are helping write a plan from scratch, you will need to sit down with the management team and understand their business in detail. You will need to pin down what opportunities it faces, and how the team expects to capitalise on them.

You will also need to find out what threats it faces, and what steps it has taken or will take to avoid them. Additional desk research may be needed into the market in general and into how the business is perceived in the marketplace by its customers.

Finally, you need to assemble detailed biographies of the main members of the management team. It can also be helpful to carry out a SWOT analysis of the business, if the management team has not done so already. SWOT stands for Strengths, Weaknesses, Opportunities and Threats – four headings that can be used to summarise a business's market position (for more on this and on other useful techniques for business and career development, see www.mindtools.com). A SWOT analysis of your own business might look something like this:

Strengths	*Weaknesses*
– Established, international client list – Reputation	– Reliant on two major clients for most of income

Opportunities	*Threats*
– Expansion into new markets – Potential to grow existing client work	– Lack of networking could lose clients – Market downturn could affect client budgets

The business plan itself needs to include the following sections:

◆ An executive summary of no more than three pages (and preferably one), which can act as a stand-alone document and sells the business to potential investors, and with a brief summary of the company's market position, prospects, plan for growth and management team.

◆ An account of the company's market positioning and the trends it hopes to exploit.

◆ A summary of the company's competitive environment, with its plans to cope with competition.

◆ A description of the business processes the company uses, plus notes on how they will be used or modified for competitive advantage.

◆ Any other factors, such as marketing or promotion, relevant to the business's plans for growth.

◆ Details of the management team and, in particular, their track record in running and growing businesses in the past.

◆ Detailed revenue, cash-flow and profit-and-loss projections spanning at least three years. These can be included as appendices.

In total, the document should not be more than about ten pages, plus appendices.

A good business plan can be worth millions of pounds for a business. If you feel you can add value to it, you should feel justified in charging a premium for the work.

4. Manuals and Technical Documents

As anyone who has struggled with a video or TV instruction book will know, clarity and simplicity are the two most important things to bear in mind when writing manuals.

Putting together this kind of material also requires, unsurprisingly, a detailed knowledge of the technology or process you are describing. Being able to test the product yourself is vitally important; make notes as you use it, not only so you can describe what to do, but also so you can describe what to do if things go wrong.

It is likely you may have to work closely with a graphic designer. Where possible, rely on pictures rather than words to describe processes as they are clearer and easier to understand.

Beyond advice already covered in Chapter 8 about writing clearly, the exact nature of each technical writing job is likely to depend on the type of product involved. If possible, I would advise trying to get hold of either an earlier version of the manual or a similar document from a competitor, and using it to look for areas that could be improved.

5. Presentations

Presentations have become an integral part of many businesses and business processes, and are used in situations that range from internal communications briefings to sales pitches to shareholder meetings. The vast majority of presentations nowadays are created using a computer program called Microsoft PowerPoint, but there is a tendency towards more sophisticated audiovisual packages incorporating video and animation on intranets or CD-ROM. Basic presentations may consist of little more than a few bullet points on some slides adorned with clip art, and are usually produced in-house. Nevertheless, there are occasional opportunities for copywriters in this area. You may be asked, for example, to create a PowerPoint version of some work carried out elsewhere; or edit an existing presentation; or even put one together as a stand-alone project. Needless to say, you will need to have access to PowerPoint for this kind of work. At the time of writing, the package costs around £300 on its own (more if you need it for an Apple Mac) but you can usually have it bundled in with other software when you buy your computer.

You will be unsurprised to know that the basic skill in writing or editing presentations is to have a good idea of who the communication is aimed at, and what will appeal to them. All too often, for example, pitch presentations stick to the following format: 'here's who we are', 'here's what we do', 'here's how we do it', 'here's what we can do for you', 'here's what it could mean for your business'. Personally, I would be amazed if this approach ever worked. The people who have to sit through these presentations are usually busy executives. Their first concern is likely to be 'what's in this for me?' not 'who are these guys?', although I would not be surprised if that question popped up too after ten minutes of a traditional presentation.

I usually advise turning the traditional pitch presentation structure on its head, so that it reads something like this: 'here's what we can do for you', 'here's how we do it', 'here's who we are so you know you can trust us'. This should, hopefully, get the audience's attention right from the off.

> **Other types of presentation may require slightly different structures but the bottom line is always: work out what is most relevant to the audience and say it up front. Leave the hows and the whos until later.**

Other tips

Here is a list of other things to do that will not only enhance the look and readability of your presentation, but also make it easier for the presenter to run through.

◆ Stick to between three and six bullet points per slide.

◆ Avoid background colours that clash or disguise text or images.

◆ Keep to a consistent style throughout your presentation, with fixed sizes and fonts for headlines and body copy.

◆ Make all points roughly the same length – say, one or two lines each.

◆ Avoid headlines of more than one line.

◆ Avoid bullet points of three lines or more unless they are there for good reason, for example as a stand-alone quote.

◆ Try to present data in the form of charts and diagrams rather than tables.

◆ Beware of vastly complicated diagrams that are difficult to read and convey little information.

◆ Use animation intelligently to improve the impact of each point and stick to a common animation theme throughout the presentation.

6. Speech Writing

Writing good speeches is an art for which people get paid a lot of money, not least because a great speech has the potential to move people far more profoundly than almost any other form of communication. (Let's face it: politicians do not make it to power by writing great newspaper articles.) Much of this power, however, comes from the delivery rather than the substance of a speech.

Great speakers recognise that their best material comes from the heart and, if they employ a scriptwriter at all, will usually insist on polishing off the final draft themselves to inject something of their own personality into it.

At a lower level, however, clients often resort to writers to help them come up with material for events such as conferences, presentations and networking sessions. When taking a brief for this kind of work, you need to find out how detailed the draft needs to be. Some speakers prefer to ad-lib off the back of a set of detailed notes or bullet points. Others need a word-by-word script. Also check to see what other materials the speaker will be using, in case you need to reference them in the speech. If you can, interview the speaker on their chosen subject so that you can ascertain their line of thought and pick up on any favourite phrases.

Wake the audience up

Next you need to be aware of what makes a good speech. For a start, as is the case with so many other forms of writing, it has to capture the audience's attention with a simple, strong emotional message right at the beginning.

This is why many speakers kick off with a joke. They are not trying to appear funny, but they know that laughing is a gut reaction and if they can raise a chuckle they have secured an emotional response. Other ways of engaging the audience can include posing a topical question, making a controversial assertion or bringing up a well-known quote. I have even seen speakers ask their audience to stand up and interact with each other in some way. This is the last thing a group of passive listeners wants to do, so it forces a strong emotional response; the audience may sit back down thinking 'What was all that about? This had better be worth it . . .', but by now, at least, they are all ears.

Keep them awake

After giving the audience a jolt that gets their attention, the speaker then needs to hold onto it for the main part of the speech. Here, the key is to map out each step in the argument and phrase it in clear, simple language. As a writer, you may have little or no control over the way your speech is delivered; stick to short, familiar words so that each point can be understood even if the speaker ends up mumbling through a faulty mike. And avoid long, technical terms that might trip up the person on the stage.

Remember, also, that you are writing spoken words. Your speech needs to read like a script, with bridges, asides and references. Also, like a script, it needs to contain occasional prompts and jolts to make sure the audience does not drift off. Ask rhetorical questions. Raise unusual examples. Above all, talk *to* the audience, not *at* them. Use phrases like 'what would you do?' and 'you've all been in a situation where . . .'

Leave them wanting more

Unlike, say, writing for the press, where you leave your least important information till last, a speech is an event – and you want to go out with a bang, not a whimper. The ending is every bit as important as the beginning.

The best way to achieve a grand finale is to quickly repeat the main points in your argument (but make it quick – no more than a few seconds) – then deliver The Big Message. This is the key point of the whole speech, summarised in a single line. Get controversial. Needless to say, you are looking to get an emotional response from your audience.

The Big Message has to hit them in the gut, not the brains. Nothing is too strong. Instead of: 'So, you see, our industry will have to adapt to these changes or face the consequences,' how about: 'If your business is ready to adapt, then I'll see you back here next year. If not, I'd advise you to start looking for a new job, now.'

Other considerations

When preparing your copy, rehearse it out loud and time yourself to make sure it is the right length. Studies have shown that the average audience has an attention span of 1,000 seconds – just over quarter of an hour. Try to keep your speech to within this time and leave the rest of the presentation for questions.

Also, pay attention to the layout of your draft. Put copy into a single column down the side of the page, so it is easier to read, and highlight key words and phrases in bold or italics. If the presentation involves slides or other props, show clearly to which ones different paragraphs relate.

> **Speech writing is a rare skill which makes a lot of demands on the writer and commands a premium in the marketplace. Once you have taken on a number of projects in this area you will be able to get a feel for the kinds of charges you can demand, but in the first instance I would suggest quoting two or three times what you would normally ask for a standard writing job of a similar size.**

7. Video Scripts

The rising popularity of video, thanks to broadband distribution, has led to an increasing demand for scripts among corporate clients. Typically, a client might want to shoot a short video that will go on their website, be distributed internally via an intranet, or be shown at events such as sales conferences. The kinds of scriptwriting assignments you could be called upon to produce might range from voiceovers for simple animated presentations to full scripts for expensive productions. Some tips for handling this kind of work include:

◆ Be aware of timing. Do not go much over 100 words of speech per minute. Most corporate videos are only about three or four minutes long at most (as anything longer costs too much and causes viewers to drift off), so you are looking at about 400 words at most. You will find it quite challenging to get everything you want to say into that word count. So aim for a miracle of direct, concise communication and cut out anything that sounds vaguely technical or waffly.

◆ In the same vein, make sure the language you use is as simple, direct and colloquial as possible. Remember your audience cannot go back and read a line again if they don't get it first time, so make sure they get it first time. Use short words and everyday language. Write as you would speak. Switch on the TV or radio news and listen to the way that newsreaders explain complex subjects, then try to do the same.

◆ Think in pictures. Even if you know the budget does not stretch to exotic locations or special effects, try to think of props, backdrops and ways to liven up your video so it does not end up as a talking head speaking to the camera. Similarly, if your video has to explain something very complex, like the offside rule in soccer for instance, then see if it is possible to do this visually rather than having to explain it in the narrative.

◆ Keep to a standard script format for your copy. Use a large, easily readable font such as 12-point Courier. Double-space your text. Break up the copy into lots of paragraphs.

◆ Re-read your text out loud when you have finished drafting it. The chances are you will find a whole bunch of phrases that are virtually impossible to say properly. Break them apart and re-work them until they sound right. Also watch out for missing words, words that might be difficult to pronounce and other possible traps for the speaker or narrator. Consider phonetic spelling for tricky or unfamiliar names.

◆ By all means, use stage directions, but do not overdo them. Turning the script into a video is someone else's job – you just take care of making sure the words are right.

See as well my comments on speech writing (above) and TV advertising in Chapter 10, which the notes above also apply to.

8. Other Types of Writing

There are almost limitless types of projects you could be called upon to handle as a writer, spanning industries as diverse as book publishing and film. Going into all of them is beyond the scope of this book. But it is safe to say that the basics of copywriting that will help you establish your business will also stand you in good stead to take on almost any contract that comes your way.

18

Beyond Copywriting

1. Where Next?

Halfway through writing this book, I upped sticks and left the UK to live in Spain. It was a lifestyle decision, but one that was made possible purely because of the nature of my work. At the time of writing, my business is healthier than ever. The only real change is that most of my contact with my British clients is over the phone rather than face to face.

The point of this story is that it illustrates how running your own copywriting business, whilst fulfilling in itself, can also provide a springboard to many other opportunities. This chapter is all about answering the question: once my business is established, what happens next?

I shall not pretend to be able to answer that question in full, but hopefully the following paragraphs will give you some pointers on the direction your business could take in future.

> If you want to expand your business, you face two options: look at ways of increasing the range and/or value of the services you offer, or expand by taking on partners or staff. Both can often be easier if you cultivate skills in a particular industry.

2. Sticking To Your Guns

The easiest option if you have a successful copywriting business is to stick with it. You may well be happy with your level of income and the lifestyle your work provides. If you are concerned about future prospects, bear in mind that your earning potential is likely to go up in line with your experience in particular fields. As you become more adept and efficient at producing copy, you will find that you can fit more projects into your schedule and so boost your overall income. Plus your network of contacts will grow over time, so you will see more referrals.

A final point worth making is that, strange though it may sound, being a self-employed copywriter can be more secure than having full-time employment in times of recession. At the turn of the millennium many of my friends with jobs in the marketing, media, new media and creative industries were made redundant as a result of the downturn in advertising and technology. I, too, found it harder to get work, but at least I had a range of clients to provide me with income, instead of a single paymaster.

3. Consultancy

As your knowledge of the trade and its related industries grows, you may find you can progress from providing copywriting services to consultancy. The difference between the two is that consultancy is usually concerned with elements of strategy, while service is concerned with delivery of specific campaigns or projects. Strategic issues may include, for example, the development of coherent guidelines for communications across a business; the formulation of policies and processes governing internal and external communications; or the introduction of new communications channels, such as websites or magazines. Because these initiatives may have a wide-ranging impact on the client's business, the consultant is usually seen as providing greater value than the service provider, and can therefore charge more.

Moving into consultancy takes a degree of confidence in one's abilities plus a fair amount of luck in spotting opportunities in the market. It is not necessarily a guarantee of stable income, either, since the demand for consultancy can fluctuate widely and communications is an area that is not often considered worthy of outside help. In the long run, you may find that it is best to provide consultancy along with your normal copywriting services and offer either to clients as the opportunity arises.

4. Marketing

Another potential spin-off from your copywriting business is the ability to offer wider marketing support. This can be particularly valuable to start-up companies that do not have an in-house marketing person or team. To provide solid advice, however, you may need to have more than just copywriting skills; experience in managing wider marketing campaigns can be important if you are to be sure you can handle logistical, legal and other issues. With luck, you may be able to work on projects that give you exposure to this kind of activity in the course of your copywriting career.

5. Brand and Corporate Identity

With experience in identifying target markets and learning how to communicate with them, you may find that you are well qualified to work on wider projects relating to branding and corporate identity. Most businesses rightly place great value on their name, company logo and any attendant strap lines or descriptors. Being involved in branding or re-branding exercises can be highly rewarding but requires painstaking research and in-depth knowledge of areas such as copyright – one reason why large corporate identity projects are usually handled by specialist agencies that are able to charge a premium for their services.

Further down the line, however, there are opportunities for copywriters in terms of the development of corporate materials that reflect the newly-created corporate ethos.

> **If you are seriously interested in breaking into this area, it is worth teaming up with a graphic design team so that you can offer a full service to clients.**

6. Setting Up Your Own Agency

The most obvious path to follow once your business has proved a success is to expand it in the traditional manner, taking on staff or partners to absorb extra work and increase profits. Expansion of a pure copywriting business can be problematic, however, which is one reason why large copywriting agencies are pretty rare.

For a start, copywriters tend to be chosen on the basis of individual skills and your clients might not appreciate you handing their work on to a colleague or subordinate. The margins involved in supplying copy, while ample for an individual or a small business, might not be sufficient to support additional staff. And it is easier to build a brand if you are recognised in having expertise in one of the industries that consumes copy, such as advertising, direct mail, the web, journalism or public relations.

If you can claim particular expertise in one of these areas and want to expand your business, it might be an idea to consider setting up an advertising, direct mail, web, press or public relations agency that can provide copywriting as part of a range of services relevant to the industry.

7. Creative Writing

Copywriting does not provide, as such, a route into creative writing. However, if you are keen to write novels, movie scripts and the like, there can be distinct advantages to starting out as a copywriter. To begin with, you will already be working with words and so will have had to grapple with many of the minutiae of the writer's trade, from managing your own time to learning what you can and cannot offset against tax. You will also be accustomed to pitching your written work, which can be a great help when submitting your first manuscript. You will be used to writing quickly and meeting deadlines. Importantly, too, the fact that you are already a professional writer might count in your favour when contacting editors. The only drawback in working as a copywriter is that you might find you are heartily sick of the keyboard by the time you sit down to bash out your opus.

Unless you are churning out best-seller material, however, beware that it could be some time before your income from creative writing matches what you get from commercial copywriting. Do not give up your day job!

Sources and References

These sources of information are far from exhaustive – each will probably lead you on to a number of others. Included here are reference sources and organisations that I have mentioned in the text and that you may find useful or essential in setting up your business, plus any other sources that I have come across in the course of my work that I think may be of interest to you.

Please note that some of these sources (websites particularly) may cease to be available as time passes. If you find this is the case, or come across other references that you think are equally useful, then please let me know by emailing me at mail@jasondeign.com, so that I can update this section in future editions of this book. Also, you might want to have a look at my own website, www.jasondeign.com, for other, more up-to-date reference sources.

Finally, bear in mind that a listing in this section does not constitute an endorsement!

Chapter 1: Why Become A Copywriter?

For background information, training and more you might want to contact the **Institute of Copywriting**, Overbrook Business Centre, Poolbridge Road, Blackford, Wedmore, Somerset BS28 4PA. Tel: (019) 3471 3563. Fax: (019) 3471 3492. Web: www.inst.org/copy

Chapter 2: Getting Started

Her Majesty's Revenue and Customs (HMRC) offers tax and employment advice and has local offices all around the country – the nearest one to you will be listed in the phone book. The department's website is at www.hmrc.gov.uk

Companies House is at Crown Way, Maindy, Cardiff CF14 3UZ. Tel 0870 3333636. Web: www.companieshouse.gov.uk, www.companieshouse.co.uk

Most internet portals incorporate **domain name registration** services which allow you to see whether the online name you want to register for your business is available.

Other **sources of advice** are banks (if you open a business account you will be offered the services of a business adviser), Business Link (www.businesslink.org, a national network of advice centres for small businesses) and the Federation of Small Businesses at www.fsb.org.uk

See **also** www.britishchambers.org.uk for your local Chamber of Commerce; the Department for Business, Enterprise and Regulatory Reform (www.berr.gov.uk); www.smallbusiness.co.uk; www.smallbusinessadvice.org.uk; www.j4b.co.uk for information on grants for business and industry; and www.startups.co.uk for start-up grants. Most of these sources of information are free of charge, but some may require a subscription fee, so do check first. Lastly, do not forget to look up trade associations and fellow business owners for advice.

Chapter 3: Getting Kitted Out

For **computers** and **peripherals** see the websites of the major manufacturers – www.apple.com, www.hp.com, www.dell.com, www.sony.com and so on – or online shops like www.buy.com or www.argos.co.uk or search a shopping comparison engine like www.kelkoo.co.uk

Microsoft: www.microsoft.com

Other **useful websites** for handling online material are: www.winzip.com (for unpacking compressed files downloaded from the internet), www.adobe.com (for Adobe Acrobat Reader, a program which is used to view documents over the net) and www.real.com (for RealPlayer, which is required to view video clips or listen to audio files from sources such as the BBC).

Webmail providers include www.hotmail.com, www.yahoo.com, www.lycos.com, www.gmail.com and others. If you have a website, check to see if your web hosting company offers web mail.

Antivirus software can be obtained from www.mcafee.com, www.symantec.com or www.sophos.com

The **Zone Alarm** firewall can be downloaded from www.zonealarm.com

For the latest on **internet service providers**, consult a specialist magazine such as *Web User*, a monthly publication from IPC (subscriptions: 0845 676 7778).

Chapter 4: Where To Work

For **serviced offices**, look in your local *Yellow Pages* under Office Rental, or go through a large national company such as Regus (www.regus.com).

Details of **IR35** can be found on the HMRC website, www.hmrc.gov.uk/ir35/ and various other sources. The AccountingWEB site, www.accountingweb.co.uk, has a large amount of information on the subject, as do many of the sites belonging to large accountancy firms; a search for 'IR35' on a search engine such as Google (www.google.com) will uncover the main ones.

Chapter 5: Book Keeping for Copywriters

See entries under previous chapters for the contact details for organisations such as HMRC.

The Motley Fool (www.fool.co.uk) has information on **pensions** and other financial products.

If you are worried about **managing cash flow**, the Better Payment Practice Group has lots of information about your statutory rights and advice on how to make sure you are paid on time. It has several publications which can be downloaded from www.payontime.co.uk or ordered on (0870) 150 2500.

Chapter 6: How To Find Work – and Keep It

Online work exchanges include Guru (www.guru.com), E-lance (www.elance.com) and Smarterwork (www.smarterwork.com); these are all US sites which, nevertheless, may offer UK and European work.

For **website hosting**, try your internet service provider. The hosting service I use at the time of writing is provided by UK2 (www.uk2.net). It is dirt cheap but offers an appalling service; approach at your peril!

For **building websites**, try *Teach Yourself HTML Visually* by Ruth Maran (Hungry Minds, ISBN 0-7645-3423-8), available from Amazon (www.amazon.co.uk); further tips on HTML and other web programming languages can be found at www.w3.org

Web authoring software packages include Fusion from NetObjects (www.netobjects.com) and WebEditor from Namo (www.namo.com).

Other online resources for **website design** include Jakob Nielsen's Alertbox (www.useit.com/alertbox) and the Yale Style Manual (http://info.med.yale.edu/caim/manual/); if you are uploading your own web pages you will also need a file transfer protocol (FTP) program from a company such as Ipswitch (www.ipswitch.com – no relation to the UK town of the same name!).

Freelance agencies online include Xchangeteam (www.xchangeteam.com) in the UK.

In the London area, **try also** Stopgap (Goodwin House, 5 Union Court, Richmond, Surrey TW9 1AA; tel: (020) 8332 0066, fax: (020) 8332 2747, www.stopgap.co.uk) and Major Players (73-75 Endell Street, London WC2H 9AJ; tel: (020) 7836 4041, fax: (020) 7836 4009, www.majorplayers.co.uk).

Finally, look out for **ads** in magazines such as *Marketing*, *Marketing Week* and *Campaign* (available from large newsagents such as WHSmiths) and

their associated websites, such as www.brandrepublic.com and
www.mad.co.uk

Pricing – for guides, speak to agencies or see the National Union of
Journalists website, http://media.gn.apc.org/feesguide/

Chapter 7: Getting Help

Professional bodies include: The Advertising Association, 7th Floor North,
Artillery House, 11-19 Artillery Row, London SW1P 1RT. Tel: (020)
7340 1100. Fax: (020) 7222 1504. www.adassoc.org.uk

The Direct Marketing Association, DMA House, 70 Margaret Street,
London W1W 8SS. Tel: (020) 7291 3300. Fax: (020) 7323 4426.
www.dma.org.uk

The Public Relations Consultants Association, Willow House, Willow Place,
Victoria, London SW1P 1JH. Tel: (020) 7233 6026. Fax: (020) 7828
4797. www.prca.org.uk

The Chartered Institute of Public Relations, 32 St James's Square, London
SW1Y 4JR. Tel: (020) 7766 3333. Fax: (020) 7766 3344.
www.ipr.org.uk

And the National Union of Journalists (see entry under Chapter 14). For a
fuller list of industry bodies, try the Marketers Portal,
www.marketersportal.com

The **Periodical Publishers Association** can be contacted at Queens House,
28 Kingsway, London WC2B 6JR. Tel: (020) 7404 4166. Fax: (020)
7404 4167. www.ppa.co.uk

Search engines worth book-marking on your browser include
www.ask.co.uk, www.google.com, www.yahoo.co.uk and
www.ukplus.com

Other **useful sites** include: www.bt.com (directory enquiries),
www.whatis.com (technical dictionary), http://babelfish.altavista.com/
(translations), http://news.bbc.co.uk/ (news) and www.ananova.com
(news).

Chapter 8: Delivering Great Copy

The basic rules of great copywriting – particularly as they apply to web copy and especially on topics such as selling benefits, not features, and using the active rather than passive voice – are covered in detail in the Grokdotcom newsletter produced by Future Now, a US internet marketing advisory publisher. To sign up, visit www.grokdotcom.com

How to Win Customers, revised edition: Heinz M. Goldmann, Pan Books Ltd, ISBN: 0330263013. This book now appears to be out of print, but may be available from second-hand bookstores or your local library.

Writing for the Web (Writer's Edition), 1st edition: Crawford Kilian, Self Counsel Press, ISBN: 1551802074. Available from Amazon.

Chapter 9: Things To Watch Out For

For **online dictionaries**, visit www.dictionary.com. Other useful sites are www.wikipedia.org and www.acronymfinder.com

Chapter 10: Writing for Advertising

The main advertising **magazine** is *Campaign*. To subscribe, visit www.brandrepublic.com

For **links to a wide range of advertising-related sites**, visit the Marketers Portal at www.marketersportal.com

There is a host of good **books** worth reading if you are serious about writing for advertising. *Positioning: The Battle for Your Mind*, by Al Ries and Jack Trout (McGraw-Hill Education; ISBN: 0071373586, available from www.amazon.co.uk) is highly recommended as background reading on brand positioning. *No Logo* (Naomi Klein, Flamingo, ISBN: 0006530400, also available from Amazon) provides further interesting insights into the brand phenomenon.

Fear of Persuasion: A New Perspective on Advertising and Regulation, by John E. Calfee (Agora, ISBN: 2940124027), is a must-read on **how advertising works**, if you can get hold of it.

Scriptwriting sites include Simply Scripts (www.simplyscripts.com).
Scriptware script formatting software is available at www.scriptware.com
Story, by Robert McKee, is published by Methuen (ISBN: 0413715604)
and available from www.amazon.co.uk

Chapter 11: Writing for Direct Mail

Direct Marketing Association: DMA House, 70 Margaret Street, London
W1W 8SS. Tel: (020) 7291 3300. Fax: (020) 7323 4426.
www.dma.org.uk
The **Royal Mail website** is at www.royalmailgroup.com

Chapter 12: Writing for Internal Communications

Compared with other copywriting disciplines, there is scant reference
material on internal communications. As a first port of call, however, get
in touch with the **British Association of Communicators in Business**
(Suite GA2, Oak House, Woodlands Business Park, Linford Wood,
Milton Keyes MK14 6EY. Tel: 01908 313 755. Fax: 01908 313 661.
www.cib.uk.com), which among other things can offer listing in its
directory of freelance copywriters.

Chapter 13: Writing for the Internet

If you are serious about **online copywriting** then I would recommend you
buy the excellent *Writing for the Web* by Crawford Kilian (Self-counsel
writing series, ISBN 1 55180 207 4), available from Amazon
(www.amazon.co.uk). The book contains details of a number of sites that
are useful to freelance writers.
Future Now's **Grokdotcom** newsletter is another must for web copywriters;
www.grokdotcom.com

Chapter 14: Writing for the Press

In the first instance, for **general information**, contact the National Union of Journalists at Headland House, 308 Gray's Inn Road, London WC1X 8DP. Tel: (020) 7278 7916. Fax: (020) 7837 8143; or visit http://media.gn.apc.org/flindex.html

For copies of *The Freelance*, contact the London Freelance Branch of the National Union of Journalists at the address above.

Contact the UK *Press Gazette* at 6-14 Underwood Street, London N1 7JQ. Tel: (020) 8269 7828. Fax: (020) 7566 5769, or visit www.pressgazette.co.uk

For more on **feature writing**, read *Writing Feature Articles: a practical guide to methods and markets*, by Brendan Hennessy (Focal Press, ISBN: 0240514718).

Chapter 15: Writing for Public Relations

See the **professional bodies** listed under Chapter 7. For other general information, try also the International Public Relations Association (IPRA), 1 Dunley Hill Court, Ranmore Common, Dorking, Surrey RH5 6SX. Tel: 01483 280 130. Fax: 01483 280 131.

Chapter 16: Writing for Sales and Sales Promotion

The **Institute of Sales Promotion** is at Arena House, 66-68 Pentonville Road, Islington, London N1 9HS. Tel: (020) 7837 5340. Fax: (020) 7837 5326. www.isp.org.uk.

A number of design **magazines** regularly cover this area, and Centaur's *In-Store Marketing* is specifically devoted to point-of-sale material. See www.mad.co.uk for details.

Chapter 18: Beyond Copywriting

For information on **expanding your business** or setting up an agency, see the entries above for professional bodies and Business Link; talk also to your bank and your accountant, if you have one.

Index